THE
JEWELRY REPAIR
MANUAL

R. ALLEN HARDY

Former Technical Editor, The American Horologist and Jeweler
Former Instructor, The Bowman Technical School

Second Edition

With illustrations by the author

 VAN NOSTRAND REINHOLD COMPANY
NEW YORK   CINCINNATI   TORONTO   LONDON   MELBOURNE

First published in paperback in 1982
Copyright © 1956, 1967 by Van Nostrand Reinhold Inc.
Library of Congress Catalog Card Number 67-18068
ISBN 0-442-23680-8

Van Nostrand Reinhold Company Inc.
135 West 50th Street, New York, NY 10020

Van Nostrand Reinhold
Latrobe Street
Melbourne, Victoria 3000, Australia

Van Nostrand Reinhold Company Ltd.
Molly Millars Lane, Workingham, Berkshire, England
RG11 2PY

Macmillan of Canada
Division of Gage Publishing Limited
164 Commander Boulevard
Agincourt, Ontario M1S 3C7, Canada

Cloth edition published 1967 by Van Nostrand Reinhold
Company

16   15   14   13   12   11   10   9   8   7   6   5   4   3   2

To
My wife, Jeanne
My son, Rick
And my daughter, Ann

Preface to the Second Edition

IN THE LAST FEW YEARS the jeweler has been confronted with unprecedented competition from every direction—department stores, discount houses, ladies' specialty shops, men's shops, hardware stores, dime stores, mail order outlets, and even service stations—all attempting to sell merchandise normally regarded as jewelry store items. There appears to be no end in sight and, as a result, progressive jewelers have had to develop one field to its fullest capacity in order to preserve the confidence the general public has in a legitimate jewelry store.

This field is service—service that is so closely related to sales that the lack of it tends to discourage indiscriminate buying from odd sources. More specifically, the trend is toward developing a complete jewelry repair department, with emphasis on the setting of stones on the premises.

This revised edition is intended to help the jeweler who wishes to expand his jewelry repair department, not only to increase his volume in the repair department, but to increase his sales volume as well. Providing these services will lead to increased sales, particularly in diamonds and mountings.

This edition provides more complete information for the novice to the trade, going into detail on the more difficult skills and introducing information on ultrasonics, steam cleaning, electroplating and other important phases.

It is hoped that this revised edition will provide that extra bit of information needed to round out the knowledge and skill of the watchmaker-jeweler combination man, who will find an increasing demand for such services in today's service-scant market.

The ability to perform these services on the premises enables the jeweler to deliver repair jobs to his customers rapidly and promptly. It eliminates the bother, expense and delay in sending this work to the over-burdened trade houses. And, most important, it builds prestige while substantially increasing profits.

R. ALLEN HARDY

Jacksonville, Florida
May, 1967

Preface to the First Edition

JEWELRY REPAIR is a broad term, frequently used to cover many phases of work that should not be correctly included under it. Many professional jewelry repairman have really advanced into the highly skilled profession of jewelry making or manufacturing by doing "special order" work. To attain this, much study, training, and a certain amount of apprenticeship is required. The work is more intricate than the average run of jewelry repairing. Again, many jewelry repairmen have become specialists in stonesetting, doing this work exclusively, thereby eliminating themselves as jewelry repairmen. They should be classed as stonesetters.

This book deals with jewelry repair in the generally accepted sense of the word—a jewelry repairman being one who repairs all types of jewelry in addition to setting precious stones. Not only are these qualifications an asset in one's own business, but they are especially desirable to an employer in today's jewelry store.

In preparing this book the most important phases have been selected, and procedures have been illustrated and explained in consecutive operations. In this way the student or beginner will not only learn the fundamentals of repairing, but with a degree of mechanical aptitude and foresight should be able to accomplish the more advanced work with ease.

It has been the authors' experience that beginners need instruction dealing with methods and procedures rather than principles and theory. Principles and theory can be easily explained and understood, but methods and procedures must be shown. For example, typical questions that are always in the mind of the beginner are: What tools do I use? How do I hold them? Just how is it done? Rarely does the "Why" type of question arise. With this in mind, the book has been constructed with special emphasis on methods and procedures to bring the beginner up to and through the finishing stages of becoming a successful jewelry repairman.

Contents

Chapter 1

Tools and Equipment and Their Uses

GENERALLY SPEAKING, if money is to be spent towards equipping a jewelry repair department, the best possible equipment should be purchased, for many reasons. Good equipment rarely breaks down when needed most and is usually the least expensive in the final analysis, lasting longer and costing less to maintain. The best equipment is usually the most versatile as opposed to cheap equipment which often will not perform the very job for which it was purchased.

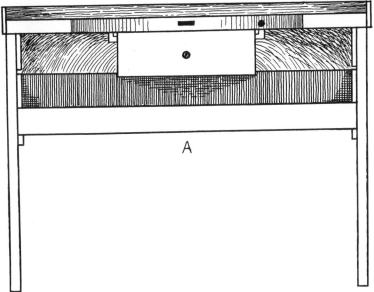

A

FIG. 1.1.   Pattern for a jeweler's bench: *A*, front.

1

At the end of this chapter there will be found a list of all the tools that the beginner must have and learn to use. Many of the items might be purchased by one who has no previous knowledge or experience with the tools. There are, however, many items which should be carefully selected, especially the heavy equipment. Accordingly we open our discussion of tools and equipment with a survey of the prime points of consideration in selecting important items.

The Jeweler's Bench

The construction and general design of the jeweler's bench (Figs. 1.1, 1.2) is of great importance. Tools and bench attachments should be placed at the handiest spot, and the design should

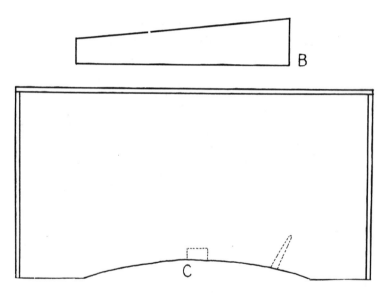

Fig. 1.2.   Pattern for a jeweler's bench: *B*, side view; *C*, top view.

follow out this idea. A strong, well-made bench is a necessity because the nature of the work demands an absence of vibration. To insure this, the bench may be secured to the floor.

The jeweler's bench as purchased from supply houses will have the following general specifications: length, 45 inches; depth, 24 inches; height to working surface, 38 inches.

Many shops build their own benches (especially when more than one are used) and dimensions may vary. In constructing jeweler's benches the following dimensions and plan will assure a satisfactory result (see Fig. 1.1A).

The top of the bench should be at least $1\frac{1}{2}$ inches thick, 21 inches wide, $2\frac{1}{2}$ feet long and 3 feet from the floor. A drawer should be fitted and attached to the top of the bench. Its length across the front should measure 16 inches; its depth $3\frac{1}{2}$ inches. This drawer must operate entirely free from the lower drawer or lap pan.

The lap pan is lined with zinc and should be fitted about 2 feet from the floor; it should run the entire length and width of the bench. It is generally made with sloping sides, starting with a $6\frac{1}{2}$-inch depth in back to a $3\frac{1}{2}$-inch depth in front (see Fig. 1.2B). Fig. 1.2C shows the shaping of the top of the bench. The front is slightly curved; the other three sides have a protective wall to prevent objects from falling from the bench.

The small drawer attached to the top of the bench may be used for keeping small tools and equipment in order. The more frequently used tools may be placed in the lap drawer. These will include mandrels, hammers, cutting shears, most-used pliers, etc. This may seem a careless arrangement for tools, but under actual working conditions, it saves time to be able to drop the hand on the wanted tool rather than select it from some remote spot when needed. The lap drawer also serves as a gold-dust collector. Filings may fall unheeded into the lap drawer and be collected later.

In the curved portion of the bench-top edge there is located a slot to receive the *bench pin* (Fig. 1.3). The bench-pin tongue is generally $\frac{1}{2}$ inch thick, $2\frac{1}{2}$ inches wide, and $1\frac{3}{4}$ to 2 inches in length, the length being the measurement running into the bench. Bench pins of this size can be obtained from supply houses.

In the average workshop there is generally a large vise available for use when needed. This is a necessity, but innumerable jobs arise that demand the use of a smaller vise. It is the author's contention that the jeweler needs a small vise (Fig. 1.32) mounted on his bench much in the same manner as on the watchmaker's bench (see Bench Vises, on page 28). The vise may be slightly larger than the one selected by the watchmaker. It will be found a great help in holding some articles to be flame-soldered, in filing, and

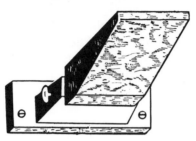

FIG. 1.3. Bench pin.

generally in holding any article when two free hands are needed. The bench vise, in a sense, becomes a third hand, and after working continuously with it, one wonders how any jeweler can work without such a vise.

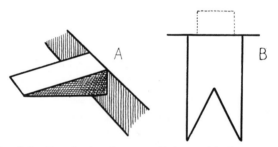

FIG. 1.4. Bench pin: *A*, as supplied; *B*, with slot cut out.

For flame-soldering, there should be an attachment or clamp secured on the right of the bench to hold the torch. The hose and nozzle should be handy, but out of the way and free of the lap drawer.

To the right of the bench pin it is convenient to locate a hole for receiving the small end of the steel ring mandrels (see Fig.

1.2C). This is handy for pounding rings, tightening bezels, and many other uses.

Along the front legs or posts of the work bench, small hooks may be attached for holding a multitude of tools, such as the ring size stick and file cleaner.

Along the inside of the bench pan, strips of heavy leather may be looped and fitted to hold pliers handily.

The bench pin, as it is received from the supply house, is shaped as shown in Fig. 1.4A. A V-shaped slot should be cut out of the

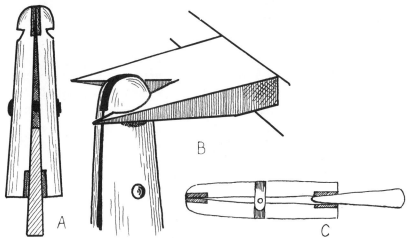

Fig. 1.5. Ring clamp: *A*, with groove at top; *B*, in working position; *C*, as supplied.

center, as shown in Fig. 1.4B. This is done to facilitate sawing and filing, and also in bracing work as shown in Fig. 1.5B. This figure shows how a ring clamp is braced against a corner of the bench with the aid of the slotted bench pin. The ring clamp has also been grooved (Fig. 1.5A) at the top, for there is no real way to brace the smooth ring clamp as it comes from the supplier (Fig. 1.5C).

Bench Block (Anvil)

Many of the small tools used by the watchmaker are equally useful to the jewelry repairman. One is the watchmaker's anvil

(Fig. 1.6) with its numerous holes and slots that offer a perfect working surface for the jeweler. This small anvil is used for riveting, flattening, and straightening various articles. In selecting a good anvil, be sure it is of correctly hardened steel that will stand plenty of abuse.

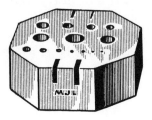

FIG. 1.6.　Bench block, or anvil

Beading Tools

Beading tools are used in forming beads when setting or tightening diamonds. The average set comes in twelve assorted sizes, complete with handle. These tools should be made of the finest

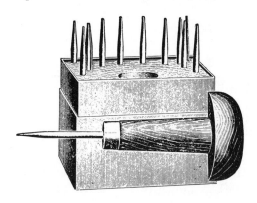

FIG. 1.7.　Beading tools.

steel, since their edges are subjected to great pressures during the forming of a bead, and inferior metal will not stand up. This is of course a perishable tool—one that will wear out through continued use.

Acid Bottles

Acid bottles (Fig. 1.8) are rather a standard type of thing. The usual design will hold only a few ounces of acid. The shoulder of the bottle and part of the cap fitting over the shoulder is of ground glass, which prevents evaporation. The stopper is also of glass, being shaped with a long taper that reaches very close to the bottom

FIG. 1.8.   Acid bottle.

of the container. It is very necessary that all acids be kept in this type of bottle, for without the protection of glass the liquid and fumes would cause serious damage. It is suggested that all bottles containing acids be correctly labeled as such.

Ultrasonic Cleaning Machines

Ultrasonic jewelry cleaning machines available to the jeweler are very efficient and the choice is varied. There is the compact, counter-size (tank and generator combined) that will clean jewelry while the customer is waiting (see Fig. 1.9); there are the larger, shop units with separate tank and generator. The shop units are more powerful and are designed for heavy duty (Fig. 1.10). Still other units are designed with tanks that are connected to the generator of the watch cleaning machine, thus saving the cost of an additional generator.

The machines offered to the jeweler on today's market are so efficient that they are considered to be essential equipment.

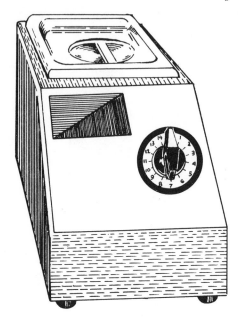

FIG. 1.9. Ultrasonic generator and tank in one unit.

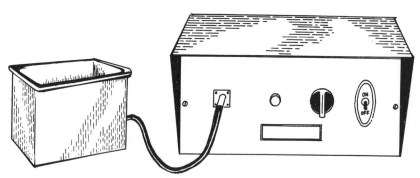

FIG. 1.10.   Heavy duty ultrasonic generator and tank.

Steam Cleaners

Steam cleaning outfits will provide a jet-type stream of hot steam that forcibly removes minute particles or film that might still be in evidence after using other methods. The steam cleaning bath is usually the last operation in the cleaning process, immediately preceding electroplating operations. When articles are not being plated, they are steam cleaned, then wrapped in tissue and delivered to the customer.

Steam cleaners are especially efficient in removing packed dirt or contamination in recesses that are impossible to reach (of course ultrasonics do the same job by way of high or low frequency vibrations).

The steam cleaner is a comparatively expensive piece of equipment (when purchasing the type used by manufacturing jewelers and trade shops) and the very small jeweler would probably not consider it unless he has a substantial jewelry repair trade. Smaller compact steam cleaners built on the principle of the pressure cooker have been offered to the trade. They are much less expensive than the standard type of steam cleaner and, although they are capable of generating a jet of steam, the main drawback to these machines is their inability to maintain pressure for a long enough period of time. They require more careful watching and regulating, while the standard jewelry steam cleaner provides live steam at any moment during a working day with much less attention.

Spring Dividers

Spring dividers (Fig. 1.11) are especially useful for ring sizing. They can be opened to the exact size of ring reduction (or expansion) and then accurately mark off the shank of the ring (for reduction) or the gold stock (for expansion). The sharp steel points make a clearly visible line on the gold which is easy to follow with the jeweler's saw.

Fig. 1.11.   Steel spring dividers.

Drawplate

A drawplate (Fig. 1.37) is used to reduce the diameter size of wire. The tip of the wire is grasped in drawing tongs and forced by a pull through the hole of diameter smaller than that of the wire. If a great reduction is desired, the wire may be drawn through several holes successively of gradually decreasing diameter. After each drawing operation the metal is annealed in order to soften it for the next reduction.

Emery Paper

As every experienced jeweler knows, emery paper has a definite place in the list of essentials, be it flat paper, shells, or flat wooden buff. Available in many different grits, emery paper is used for roughing out operations as well as for polishing. There is also a product available that is a cloth rather than a paper, and it may be purchased in the same forms that have always been available in emery paper. The cloth product has the advantage of being more durable.

Emery Ring Shells

Years ago the only ring shell available to the jeweler was the paper ring shell or cone (or buff). They were and still are useful in refinishing the inside surfaces of rings. One drawback, however, was the way they were fitted to the wooden taper spindle. About an inch from the end, the emery shells did not fit the wooden surface smoothly but were too loose. Therefore, when in use, this section could be torn or cut easily as polishing was attempted, thus rendering the shell useless. Finally, someone decided to correct the situation and today these ring shells are available to the jeweler in a cloth material (usually under a different numbering system for grit) that fits the entire wooden spindle like a glove. The cloth material is more expensive by the dozen shells but less expensive in actual use, since cloth shells last much longer than paper shells.

Both qualities of shells are available from supply houses and the beginner is advised to be conscious of differences in design as well as differences in grit designations. Average emery shells of paper quality usually range from #3 (coarse) to #4/0 (fine). The cloth quality usually ranges from 1 to 5, grit #1 being the finest and #5 the coarsest.

Files

Files come in such a wide range and such variety (Fig. 1.12) it is hard to advise the beginner precisely which files to purchase. Opinions are apt to vary, since there are a number of ways to arrive at a good polish on any article by means of files, emery, tripoli, and rouge. Files usually are purchased in a #0 to #4 range, flat, half-round, or barrette. It is hardly necessary for the jeweler to use more than two cuts of files—#2 and #4 in flats, half-round, or barrette.

A complete set of jeweler's needle files—round, square, three-square, entering, knife, half-round, crossing, and barrette—is well worth the investment. They are essential for finishing and forming small work.

The Flexible-Shaft Machine

The flexible-shaft machine (Fig. 1.13) is a very handy piece of equipment for the jewelry repairman. It should be selected with great care since it is very durable equipment that will last for many years, often requiring no attention other than occasional oiling.

The handpiece is of primary importance. There are two types to consider—the collet type and the Jacobs type of handpiece. While the collet type is very acceptable for general work, the Jacobs type is recommended for work of greater precision, such as diamond setting.

The motor for the flexible-shaft machine may be about one-tenth horsepower. It is controlled by a foot rheostat and will provide revolutions per minute of 0 to 15,000. It is usually equipped with a bail for hanging up the machine, saving valuable bench space.

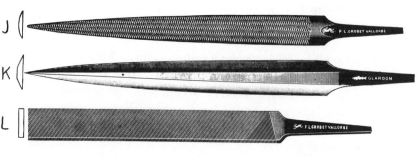

Fig. 1.12.   Files: *A*, round; *B*, square; *C* three-square; *D*, entering; *E*, knife;
F, half-round; *G*, crossing; *H*, barrette; *I*, riffle files; *J*, half-round file; *K*,
barrette file; *L*, flat file; *M*, joint file.

Flexible-shaft attachments are too numerous to mention, and of course are mounted on arbors that are of a diameter easily handled by the collet type or the Jacobs type handpiece.

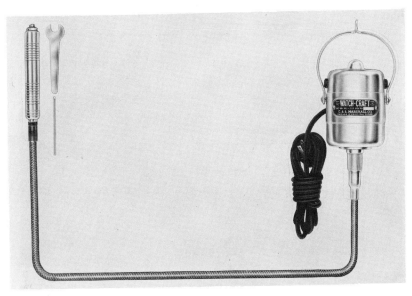

Photo, C. & E. Marshall Company

Fig. 1.13.   Flexible-shaft machine.

Hammers

Hammers (Fig. 1.14) are a very important part of the jeweler's equipment. The Swiss-style riveting hammer (Fig. 1.14A) should be selected with care. This is a delicately balanced hammer with one flat or pounding side and one wedge-shaped or riveting side. The riveting side deserves special attention. The best riveting shape is slightly rounded, with no sharp edges.

The jeweler's ball-peen hammer (Fig. 1.14B) of medium light weight is a fine little hammer for countless pounding jobs. This hammer is especially useful to jewelers employed in the metal arts and crafts field, being used in many chasing operations. The jeweler in the average jewelry store is hardly called upon to do such highly skilled work. Nevertheless, the ball-peen hammer is valuable to him for many other uses, one of them being the simple

A

FIG. 1.14.   Hammers: *A*, steel riveting hammer; *B*, ball-peen hammer.

B

pounding of a piece of gold inserted in a ring to make the size larger.

FIG. 1.15.   Bench lamp.

The Bench Lamp

The jeweler's bench lamp (Fig. 1.15) should be just as fine a lamp as the watchmaker uses, particularly if he is to set stones. A fine quality of light means a fine grade of work. Selecting a bench lamp is hardly a problem these days, since improvements are being made continually in adequate lighting. It is best to select one that will reach every section of the bench rather than one limited in range.

Loupes

The jewelry repairman does not have to use a loupe (Fig. 1.16) nearly so much as the engraver or the watchmaker, but the selection of correct loupes is just as important. For average jewelry work, the engraver's loupe (4-inch) is usually strong enough. For stonesetting, a 1½-inch to 2½-inch loupe is good. (The 4-inch is

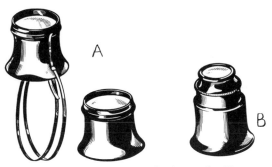

Fig. 1.16.   Loupes: *A*, single; *B*, double.

2.5-power; the 2½-inch is 4-power; the 1½-inch is 7-power.) A stronger loupe, such as 18-power, may be used for close inspection of diamonds and other critical work, but is much too strong for actual work. An 18-power loupe brings one too close to the work to allow for clearance.

Mallets

The rawhide mallet (Fig. 1.17A) is essential in pounding ring shanks into shape on the steel mandrel. After continued use the faces of the mallet lose their shape and become nicked and distorted. This is to be expected; it is the nature of rawhide to do just that, this condition being no hindrance to the usefulness of the mallet. Its purpose is to pound without damage to the ring shank, and a misshapen face does not interfere with that purpose.

If it is desired to have a mallet with a harder pounding surface or face, but one that will not damage or mar the surface of the article, then consider the fiber-faced mallet (Fig. 1.17B). This may be purchased with a 5-ounce weight and ¾-inch face and with detachable hard fiber faces.

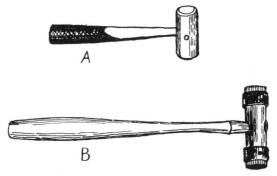

Fig. 1.17.   Mallets: *A*, rawhide; *B*, fiber-faced.

There are many other variations of mallets or hammers that the beginner or old-timer might find particularly suited to his own needs. For instance, there is the small brass mallet used by the watchmaker for staking operations, the brass and fiber-faced mallet in light and heavy weights (also a favorite of watchmakers) and the heavier ball-peen hammers. Everyone to his own liking and preference, the main consideration being skillfully and neatly executing a given job.

The Steel Marker

The steel marker (Fig. 1.18) is a finely tapered steel point mounted in a knurled handle, a very handy tool. During the course of a working day the jeweler has as much use for it as the

FIG. 1.18. Steel marker, or scriber.

watchmaker has for a bench knife. One important advantage of the steel marker is its adaptability for conversion into a first-class pin pusher. Slight alteration of the point is necessary.

Polishing Motors and Dust Collectors

A polishing motor (Fig. 1.19) is important equipment in any shop, be it watch repair or jewelry repair. Such a motor should be purchased from a jewelry supply house, not because the quality of the motors is better there, but because they are designed with the jeweler in mind.

The height of the motor (above the base), the speed, and the horsepower are of prime consideration. The height of the spindle should be about 7¼ inches. The horsepower should be ¼ plus. The revolutions per minute for a single-speed motor should be 3450; for a two-speed motor, 3450 and 1725.

Motors can be purchased with two taper spindles or with one taper spindle and one arbor spindle. These spindles, if damaged or lost, can be easily replaced through supply houses.

Dust collectors, including motors mounted over dust-collecting apparatus, are highly desirable for any shop, especially the jewelry repairman's shop, for all precious metals polished away during a given period of time are saved in the dust bags. This dust is shipped to the refiners and credit is given for the value of the gold. If enough work is done at the dust collector, this valuable piece of equipment can be more than self-supporting.

Dust collectors can be purchased in various sizes and designs. If space is limited, table models with only one spindle can be purchased. The standard type of dust collector is designed with the motor mounted over the dust-collecting apparatus, which in turn is located directly over the two dust bags.

Photo, C. & E. Marshall Company

Fig. 1.19.   Two-speed polishing motor.

The advantages of the large, standard type of dust collectors are obvious, since they keep the shop clean and the air free from harmful abrasive dust in addition to the savings earned by refining the waste collected in the dust bags.

Pliers

Most of the small hand tools need little or no discussion, although there are a few, like ring-shaping pliers, that pose quite a problem to the beginner. The half-round pliers shown in Fig. 1.20A are a must for average ring-sizing work, because with these the shank can be manipulated or shaped very quickly without marring the surfaces of the shank. Pliers with both jaws flat are incorrect for this type of work.

Another timesaver is a pair of pliers shaped as shown in Fig. 1.20B. These do a job of a more specialized nature, since they create a sharper and more definite bend in the shank. Use care in selecting pliers of this nature. The edge, as illustrated, should be rounded to prevent marring surfaces.

Another handy pair of pliers used in ring shaping is shown in Fig. 1.20C. These pliers are fundamentally designed to be bow pliers, used for tightening bows on pocket watches. The leverage is great on these pliers, and they will bend and shape the sturdiest shank.

Next, consider the ordinary snipe-nose pliers (see Fig. 1.20D). The jeweler should have two pairs of these 4½-inch pliers to handle a very simple but very important operation—the opening and closing of jump rings, links, etc. Naturally, a fine-pointed shape is desired to handle the very tiny rings as well as the larger ones. Owing to the slanted position of the two jaws of the pliers while holding an article, it is sometimes hard to keep the article from flying away, since the jaws are smooth and the article highly polished. The answer to this is not pliers with milled or rough jaws. Of course rough jaws will hold the article securely, but they will also mar it. The best way to prevent slippage is to secure snipe-nose pliers with parallel, smooth jaws. The tool is a little bulkier, but the advantages are manifold.

The flat-nose pliers of Fig. 1.20E are used for many minor operations, such as straightening articles, holding articles while they are being worked on, and general work.

Flat-nose parallel pliers are also a worthwhile tool, for they can quickly serve the purpose of a small vise, having the advantage of the twisting and turning positions made possible by holding them in the hand.

End-cutting pliers should be about 4½ to 5½ inches long and

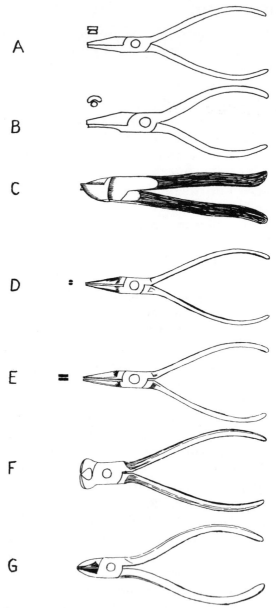

FIG. 1.20. Pliers: *A*, half-round; *B*, ring-shaping; *C*, bow; *D*, snipe-nose; *E*, flat-nose; *F*, end-cutting; *G*, side-cutting.

20

of sturdy construction (see Fig. 1.20F). Side cutters are just as important because they can frequently make a cut impossible to make with end cutters (Fig. 1.20G).

Round-nose pliers need no illustration. They are shaped exactly like snipe-nose pliers with the exception of the inside jaws, which are round instead of flat. These are useful for rounding wire and many other shaping and bending operations.

Ring Stretchers

Ring stretchers are available from numerous manufacturers and often the design is quite different. Some manufacturers offer a combination stretcher with contracting device (Fig. 1.21). Even

Fig. 1.21.   Ring sizer; enlargement and reduction of wedding rings.

the method of expanding rings will vary among manufacturers. Some will offer devices that expand the ring by rolling or pressing the shank, which is really a miniature rolling mill; others will approach the expanding operation by using pressure from the inside by way of a mandrel with split sections (Fig. 1.21). Regardless of the design employed the ring stretcher and/or contractor are a welcome addition to any shop, particularly for use on those rings that require only slight alteration. The contracting device may only be used on band or non-stone rings; stone rings must still be cut to reduce the size. Fig. 1.22 is an example of a rolling, expansion device which comes equipped with different sizes of dies to accommodate rings of all dimensions.

FIG. 1.22.   Ring stretcher, the roller method.

Saw Blades

The average run of jeweler's-saw blades (Fig. 2.3) range from size #4/0 (very fine) to #4 (very coarse). The manufacturing jeweler may find a use for each size, but the average jewelry-store technician can do well with about three sizes—fine, #3/0; medium, #1 or 1/0; and coarse, #3. These blades are very fragile and easily broken. It is advisable to carry an adequate reserve stock at all times.

Saw Frames

A jeweler's-saw frame (Fig. 2.7) should be very carefully purchased, for here is a piece of equipment that is used many times during the jewelry repairman's day. For average use a saw frame with a 2-inch depth is handiest and easiest to maneuver. It is well to have on hand frames of a greater depth, such as 4-inch and 6-inch frames. Deep frames are necessary for sawing out large plates or sections of metal for piercing work impossible to handle with the 2-inch-depth frame. Most jeweler's-saw frames are adjustable from 0 to 5 inches to accommodate whatever length of saw blade is being used.

Shears

Jeweler's shears (Fig. 1.23) are used for many miscellaneous operations, one of the most frequent being the operation of cutting off solder from the sheet. These shears should be of good steel correctly hardened. One feature to watch for in purchasing shears is freedom of operation. The joint where the two sections are put together should have the right amount of freedom, or else the scissors will be cumbersome to handle and a constant worry. It should not be so free that the handles fall together of their own

FIG. 1.23.   Jeweler's shears.

weight; neither should it be so tight that pressure interferes with the accuracy of the intended cut. If it is possible to select shears from several pairs, be sure to select the pair that meets the above qualifications.

Soldering Blocks

A soldering block (Fig. 1.24) may be purchased in asbestos or in charcoal. One material works as well as the other, the only consideration being durability. Charcoal is very light and very

FIG. 1.24.   Asbestos soldering block.

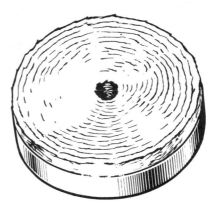

susceptible to breakage if abused. It is a good idea to anticipate this feature by wrapping the block with light binding wire. This wrapping, of course, is done around the sides. Asbestos soldering blocks are more durable and may be purchased in a variety of shapes.

The Electric Soldering Iron

An electric soldering iron (Fig. 1.25) is a useful piece of equipment for soft-soldering hard-to-get-to places and for pieces of jew-

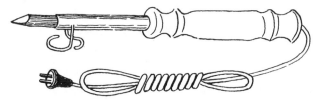

FIG. 1.25.   Electric soldering iron.

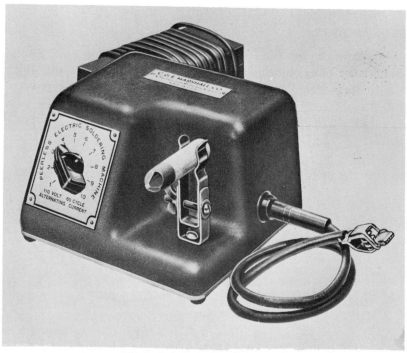

Photo, C. & E. Marshall Company

FIG. 1.26.   Electric soldering machine.

elry with delicate finishes that will not bear up under the direct heat of an alcohol flame. Such an iron may be purchased with a simple plug-in for 110-volt, 60-cycle alternating current.

The Electric Soldering Machine

Electric-arc soldering requires a completely different technique from flame soldering, and all electric machines work on the same basic principle. The most modern machines come with either a sliding rheostat or a dial-type rheostat (Fig. 1.26) that regulates the heat from zero to a degree high enough to solder platinum. It is not limited, and the most important thing to consider is the quality and durability of the machine. Electric equipment of this nature should be of the best, to avoid future trouble due to bad connections or failure during the repair of critical jobs.

Gold-Testing Needles

Gold-testing needles (Fig. 1.27) and gold-testing stones for yellow gold (Fig. 1.28) may be purchased separately or together. There are usually nine needles, ranging from 4 to 20 karats, with

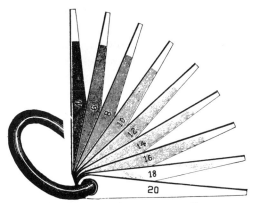

Fig. 1.27.   Gold-testing needles.

each needle numbered in 2-karat graduations. The usual way to test gold is to rub the questionable article on the gold-testing stone, and then rub about three needles of different karat value

(10K, 14K, and 18K, for example) close to the original mark. Next, using the glass stopper from the nitric acid bottle (this stopper is tapered so that the tip may be used to apply the acid in small

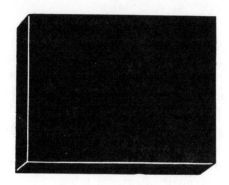

Fig. 1.28.   Testing stone.

amounts), rub a little acid over all the gold marks. The nitric acid seems to intensify the color of the gold, and the two marks most nearly matching will be readily apparent. This will determine the exact karat value or the closest to it.

The Torch

Before purchasing any flame type of soldering apparatus, it is well to be sure it will do all the work expected of it.

The oxygen-gas torch with pressure gauge (Fig. 1.29) is the most expensive and desirable of all the soldering outfits, since it has no limitations for the jewelry repairman. Desired pressure can be instantly regulated. A wide range of tips will take care of any job the jeweler might want to solder.

A fairly new device has been presented to the repairman within the past few years. This is the gas torch designed very compactly, with torch and gas chamber or cartridge all in one unit. This can be handy for a shop not having natural gas connections or access to manufactured gas. One point should be closely considered before purchasing this type of soldering outfit. Be sure your particular range of work can be handled with the flame ejected by this unit. Jewelers should have available a very tiny pointed flame that will melt or solder platinum.

Then there is the acetylene torch to consider. Acetylene has long been used for welding and soldering of all kinds, and its efficiency has been well established. The jeweler's acetylene torch

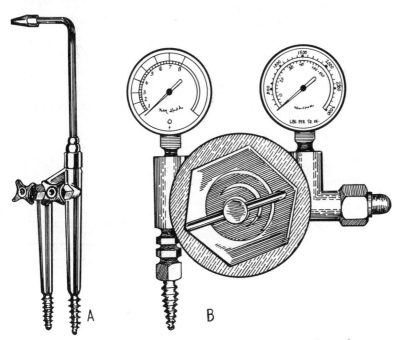

FIG. 1.29.   *A*, Oxygen-gas torch; *B*, oxygen gauge and regulator.

reaches a temperature of 2800° Fahrenheit. One can be bought with various-sized tips which project a flame of a size ranging from that of a needle point up to that of a large brush flame. The tanks can usually be furnished by local hardware stores.

Tweezers

Tweezers are important items that should be very meticulously selected, although they are fairly inexpensive. First, the jeweler should have a pair of all-purpose tweezers as shown in Fig. 1.30. As its name implies, this tool is used for picking up and handling almost anything the jeweler deals with. Actually, it is a good idea to have several pairs on hand. Some may be favored for specific operations, particularly after the points have been reworked a few

FIG. 1.30.   Tweezers, AA style.

times. Soldering tweezers are very inexpensive, and the repairman should have several pairs in different designs—especially the slide-lock style shown in Fig. 1.31. These may be 5 or 6 inches long.

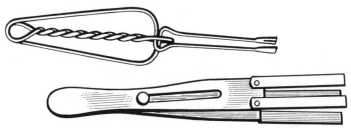

FIG. 1.31.   Soldering tweezers.

Bench Vises

Just as the watchmaker uses a small bench vise mounted on the extreme right of his bench, so should the jeweler avail himself of this very necessary piece of equipment. The jeweler's bench vise (Fig. 1.32) need not be expensive. It should be slightly larger than the watchmaker's vise. It can be used to hold a number of articles while soldering. It is a third hand, so to speak, leaving two free hands, and holds in position the pieces to be soldered until the job is done.

One of the reasons that this vise need not be of top quality is that frequently the flame may touch the surface or the heat from the article may travel through sections of the vise. A beautiful finish could be destroyed. Also, during the course of the day, much filing is done with the aid of the vise. This will soon give the vise a rather battered appearance, but does not harm its usefulness. So, bear in mind when purchasing a vise for the jeweler's bench that it does not have to be the finest.

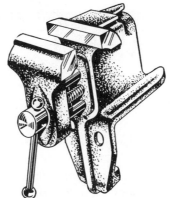

Fig. 1.32.   Bench vise.

The following alphabetical list covers all the personal tools the beginner must have, plus the essential equipment which he must learn to use but which is generally provided by the store or shop. The letter (E) marks those hand tools that are considered essential. Items such as flux and solder, though not marked with (E), are essential to the beginner and must be purchased for his practice work.

Anvil (E)   Same as *bench block* (Fig. 1.6).

Beading tools (E)   Used in stonesetting (Fig. 1.7).

Bearing burrs (E)   Used to form seats in setting stones (Fig. 13.3).

Beeswax (E)   Has many uses; particularly useful in stonesetting for picking up stones.

Bench, jeweler's   A bench of sturdy construction and special design. The outstanding features are a lap drawer or apron drawer and slots to receive the bench pin (Figs. 1.1, 1.2).

Bench block (E)   For small pounding operations, driving out pins, riveting, and many other uses (Fig. 1.6).

Bench brush (E)   Used to keep bench clean and free of dust (Fig. 1.33).

FIG. 1.33.   Bench brush.

Bench pin   For general use in filing and shaping work (Figs. 1.3, 1.4).

Blowpipe (E)   For flame-soldering (Fig. 3.3).

Borax   Used with a little water as a flux. Not essential, since satisfactory fluxes can be purchased (Fig. 3.1A).

Borax brushes, camel's-hair   Small ones are used for applying flux to joints. Larger ones are used for applying lacquer as well as other solutions (Fig. 3.1B).

Borax slate   Used with prepared stick borax to mix a paste flux for soldering (Fig. 3.1C).

Bottles, acid   Airtight glass containers to hold acids for testing metals, etc. (Fig. 1.8).

Broaches (E)   For enlarging holes, as in fitting pins to a joint and pinstem (Fig. 7.4).

Brush, brass wheel   For putting special finishes on soft metals.

Brush, steel wheel   For putting special finishes on hard metals.

Brush, washout   Used in scrubbing and cleaning various articles of jewelry (Fig. 1.34).

FIG. 1.34.   Washout brush.

Brush, watchmaker's medium stiff (E)   Used to brush and clean work while in the process of being filed, trimmed, or otherwise repaired (Fig. 1.35).

Fig. 1.35.   Watchmaker's brush.

Brushes, bristle wheel   For all types of work, small and large (Fig. 5.3).

Buff, combination felt ring and wheel   A buff specially designed to polish all surfaces of a ring without changing buffs (Fig. 5.2).

Buffs, cloth wheel   Used primarily to restore a polish with the application of polishing abrasives; available in muslin and cotton flannel (Figs. 5.4, 5.5).

Buffs, emery inside ring   Used for grinding, finishing, and polishing the inside of a ring or similar surface (Fig. 5.1).

Burnisher (E)   Used in stonesetting and to remove light scratches on metal surfaces (Fig. 13.45).

Cup, extra-large alcohol   May be used as a container for the pickle solution, cyanide, soda, or alcohol (Fig. 1.36).

Dividers, steel spring (E)   Used in ring sizing to determine the correct amount of metal to add or remove (Fig. 1.11).

Fig. 1.36.   Extra-large alcohol cup.

Drawplate, forty-hole   Used for reducing the size of round
wire (Fig. 1.37).

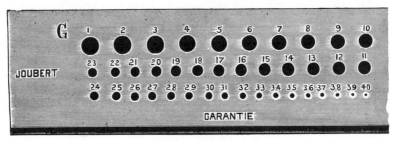

FIG. 1.37.   Forty-hole drawplate.

Drills (E)   Used in piercing, stonesetting, and general work
(Fig. 1.38).

FIG. 1.38.   Drill.

Emery paper   Available in flat sheets of various grits; for finishing, shaping, and polishing.
Emery ring shells (E)   Available in paper or cloth quality for
finishing inside surfaces of rings (Fig. 5.1).
Emery sticks (E)   For buffing by hand (Fig. 1.39).

FIG. 1.39.   Emery stick.

Files (E)   Essential are six-inch half-round, joint, barrette, and
flat files; also a set of jeweler's needle files for more delicate
work. Riffle files are convenient to reach surfaces otherwise
inaccessible (Fig. 1.12).
Flexible-shaft machine   Used in setting stones, drilling, brushing, cleaning, and polishing small recesses (Fig. 1.13).

Gravers (E)   Four are needed: #40 flat graver, #52 round graver, #1 knife-edged graver, and an onglet graver. These are used in stonesetting and various trimming operations (Fig. 12.10).

Hammers (E)   A light, steel, riveting hammer and a ball-peen hammer (Fig. 1.14).

Handles, file (E)   Many lengths, shapes, and sizes may be purchased to accommodate the many files needed by the jewelry repairman (Fig. 2.13).

Handles, graver (E)   Available in various lengths; also in full-head and half-head shapes (Fig. 12.13).

Lamp, alcohol (E)   Used in soft-soldering and in softening shellac and cement (Fig. 1.40).

FIG. 1.40.   Alcohol lamp.

Lamp, bench   Should be specially designed to bring direct light to all work in any position on the bench (Fig. 1.15).

Ligne gauge, degree (E)   Used for measuring the girdles of stones and the diameters of stonesetting burrs (Fig. 13.5).

Loupe (E)   A magnifying glass used for inspecting fine work and during delicate operations (Fig. 1.16).

Mallet (E)   Most essential is a rawhide mallet for pounding ring shanks. Fiber-faced mallets are also helpful (Fig. 1.17).

Mandrel, ring (E)   Two are needed: one steel mandrel with a groove and one steel mandrel without groove. The grooved mandrel is used working with stone rings when the culet is too low to clear the smooth mandrel. The smooth or plain mandrel is used for all other rings not having a low culet stone (Fig. 6.8).

Marker, steel (E)   Has many uses; excellent as a pin pusher (Fig. 1.18).

Milgrain tools (E)   Used in stonesetting for finishing an edge (Fig. 1.41).

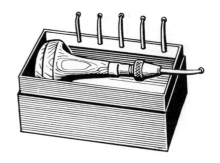

Fig. 1.41.   Milgrain tools.

Motor, polishing   For grinding, buffing, and generally polishing and finishing work (Fig. 1.19).

Oilstones (E)   For grinding and polishing tools and gravers: an India oilstone for grinding and an Arkansas oilstone for polishing (Fig. 12.14).

Pliers (E)   Bow pliers (contracting), half-round, flat snipe-nose, flat snipe-nose parallel with smooth jaws, broad parallel with rough jaws, side cutters, and end cutters (Fig. 1.20).

Polishing cloth, Selvyt   Used to restore luster to articles by hand-buffing (Fig. 1.42).

Ring clamp (E)   Used to hold rings during the setting or tightening of stones; also to hold various articles during filing or otherwise repairing (Fig. 1.5C).

Ring sizes, U.S. standard   Used to establish the correct ring size by fitting to the finger (Fig. 1.43).

Actual Size
Cross Section
of Rings

FIG. 1.42.   Selvyt cloth.   FIG. 1.43.   Ring sizes.

Rouge   An abrasive used to obtain a highly polished finish to gold, silver, platinum, etc.; available in many grades.

Saw, hack- (E)   Heavier and sturdier than the jeweler's saw; for sawing out quickly from stock metals (Fig. 2.6).

Saw blades (E)   For use with the jeweler's-saw frame; available in sizes 4 to 4/0 for general work (Fig. 2.8).

Saw frame, jeweler's- (E)   Available in many depths, usually 2-inch, 4-inch, and 6-inch; adjustable from 0 to 5 inches in blade length (Fig. 2.7).

Screwdriver (E)   Generally useful, especially in optical work (Fig. 9.1).

Sharpener, graver (E)   A holder for gravers and other tools while they are being sharpened (Fig. 12.11).

Shears (E)   For cutting solder and thin metal (Fig. 1.23).

Size gauge, ring (E)   Used to check the size of a ring before and after sizing; also in determining lengths of sizes to be put in or sizes to be taken out of rings by using a gauge located on the side of the stick near the top (Fig. 5.2).

Soldering block, asbestos or charcoal (E)   Used with blowpipe or torch. Articles are placed on the pad and soldered (Fig. 1.24).

Soldering iron, electric   Useful for many soft-soldering operations (Fig. 1.25).

Soldering machine, electric   For countless soldering operations, hard-solder and soft-solder (Fig. 1.26).

Steam cleaner   A method for cleaning jewelry using a controlled jet of hot steam. Generally useful for reaching otherwise inaccessible areas and for final cleaning operations.

Steel rod (E)   Two sizes, 2.25 mm square and 3.0 mm square; used for making punches and pushers.

Testing needles, yellow gold   Used in conjunction with a testing stone to determine the karat value of gold when the karat stamp is missing. The needles are gold tipped (Fig. 1.27).

Testing stone   See *testing needles* (Fig. 1.28).

Tongs, drawing   Used to hold wire while drawing it through a drawplate.

Torch   For flame-soldering, usually oxygen and city-gas combination (Fig. 1.29; shown with oxygen regulator).

Tripoli   A cutting abrasive used to remove file marks and scratches preparatory to the final polishing operation.

Tweezers, AA (E)   For general use in picking up small parts (Fig. 1.30).

Tweezers, soldering (E)   For holding articles during the soldering operation (Fig. 1.31).

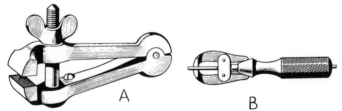

Fig. 1.44.   Hand vises: *A*, European type; *B*, American type.

Vise, bench (E)   For holding articles during filing or soldering operations. The size of the vise should be slightly larger than the watchmaker's bench vise (Fig. 1.32).

Vise, hand (E)   For holding work too large for a pin vise (Fig. 1.44).

Vise, pin (E)   Used to hold pinstems, wire during roll-filing, and other articles for alterations. An assortment of different sizes is necessary (Fig. 1.45).

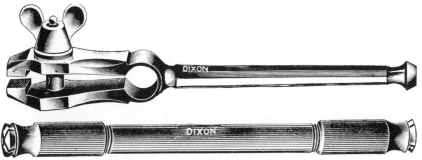

FIG. 1.45.   Pin vises.

Chapter 2

Sawing and Filing

Use of bench pin
Sawing
Filing

THE JEWELRY REPAIRMAN spends a large part of his time using the bench pin. Before beginning to saw and file, this versatile piece of equipment should be studied and prepared for use.

Use of Bench Pin

See Fig. 2.1 for an illustration of one type of bench pin available from most suppliers. This style is attached to the bench with screws. Although designs may vary slightly, this type generally has a slotted metal base in which the bench pin may be made firm with the use of a lock-screw. The advantage of this style lies in the fact that it may be attached to any surface.

Fig. 2.2 shows the ordinary tongued bench pin. This style is just right for the jeweler's bench with a built-in slot.

Now for the shaping of the bench pin. It is true that the bench pin can be used to good advantage just as it is, without any alteration. In fact, it would be well to have two bench pins on hand—one not altered and one shaped as seen in Fig. 2.3. The job at hand would indicate the one to be used.

The V-shape shown in Fig. 2.3 makes it possible to perform a vast number of different sawing and filing operations as well as providing a very adequate brace for the ring clamp. Note that the bench pin is shown in the inverted position in Fig. 2.4. This fur-

FIG. 2.1. Bench pin with metal bench attachment.

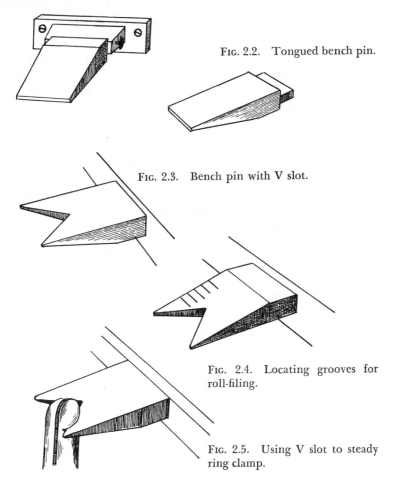

FIG. 2.2. Tongued bench pin.

FIG. 2.3. Bench pin with V slot.

FIG. 2.4. Locating grooves for roll-filing.

FIG. 2.5. Using V slot to steady ring clamp.

nishes a different filing plane as opposed to the straight position shown in Fig. 2.3.

Since the jeweler is called upon to do a considerable amount of roll-filing, what better surface can be found than the bench pin? Of course there are filing blocks held in vises reserved for this operation (the usual watchmaker's technique), but the jewelry repairman has little time to set up special equipment during a busy day. Several notches, of different sizes and depths, placed on the left of the bench pin (see Fig. 2.4) will serve the repairman well and accommodate any and all pins for roll-filing.

Fig. 2.5 shows how the bench pin may be an invaluable aid in bracing the ring clamp during an operation where the work must be firm and steady. Fig. 2.11 shows how a piece of metal may be placed in position for sawing, an advantage made possible only by altering the bench pin to a V-shape. Fig. 6.10 shows how the hand may steady a ring placed on the bench pin for the inside filing operation. Of course, this operation could be just as easily accomplished using the unaltered bench pin.

Fig. 6.11 shows how easily the sides of a ring may be filed by using one side of the V-shaped bench pins. As the filing progresses, the ring is turned in the fingers until all surfaces are evenly dressed down. Fig. 6.13 shows how the tip of the bench pin may be used to steady the ring. Fig. 6.18 shows another important operation, the squaring off of a piece of sizing stock.

Sawing

A small hacksaw (Fig. 2.6) and a regular jeweler's saw (Fig. 2.7) will cover the jeweler's needs for average work. The hacksaw is

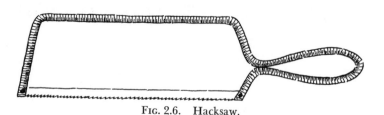

Fig. 2.6.   Hacksaw.

used mainly for speedy sawing such as cutting pieces out of sheet metal or from rods and bars. The blade (Fig. 2.8B) has more height than the jeweler's-saw blade (Fig. 2.8A). This is to give it

FIG. 2.7.   Jeweler's saw frame.

additional strength for heavier work and faster sawing. Because of this height all sawing must be done in a straight line. In adjusting a blade into the frame, the teeth should point forward, away from the handle. In use, the cutting stroke is away from the operator.

FIG. 2.8.   Saw blades: *A*, jeweler's-saw blade; *B*, hacksaw blade.

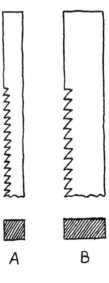

A   B

Using the jeweler's saw (Fig. 2.8A) requires more delicate handling and greater skill. The blade is adjusted by first tightening the screw controlling the length of the frame. Placing the saw in the upper clamp, tighten, with the teeth pointing towards the lower clamp. Placing the upper end of the frame against the edge of the bench, and resting the handle lightly against the body of the operator, add a little pressure to the saw frame by bending the body forward and tightening the saw in the lower clamp. This provides tension, eliminating any slack.

In sawing a flat piece of stock, the correct saw blade must be selected. Fig. 2.9 shows what will happen should a large blade be selected for a thin piece of metal. The distance between the saw teeth should always be less than the thickness of the metal, so that two or more teeth are in action against the metal (Fig. 2.10).

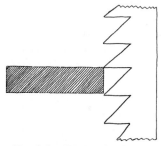

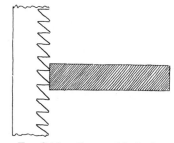

FIG. 2.9.   Wrong blade size.   FIG. 2.10.   Correct blade size.

Jeweler's-saw frames may be obtained with different depths, since it is often necessary to saw around corners and curves. For example, it would be possible to maneuver a saw with a 12-inch depth from many angles on a large piece of stock, while with a 2½-inch depth, sawing would be limited to the depth of the frame and maneuverability severely curtailed.

By drilling a hole within the edge of a piece of metal, the saw blade may be inserted and reclamped to the lower clamp. In this manner sawing may be started at any point within the metal. This is called *piercing*.

To start sawing, stroke the metal upward with light pressure. Two or three strokes will do, and the regular sawing action may be begun (see Fig. 2.11). The cutting is done on the downward

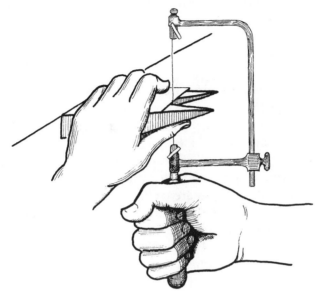

Fig. 2.11.   Using the jeweler's saw.

stroke; as the hand is pulled downward, add a little forward pressure. The upward stroke should receive no real pressure, but should be allowed to slide lightly in position over the metal. A little beeswax applied to the blade will avoid jamming and prevent breakage.

To cut a straight line, keep the saw blade perpendicular to the flat metal piece. In this manner, control in following the line as the blade advances may be gained. Crooked sawing usually results from deviation from the perpendicular.

To turn a corner the blade must be rotated slowly, not cutting until the full turn is made. Be sure the blade moves freely before progressing forward.

Skillful sawing in following a line closely will eliminate much filing. This skill can be acquired only through continued practice. A skillful worker rarely breaks blades. They are replaced when worn dull.

When blades break near the top or bottom, the saw frame may be shortened and continued use may be gotten from the blade. If the blade is broken short, it is best to discard it and insert a new one.

Filing

Good filing is essential in jewelry work. Not only should a minimum of filing be done, to save time and unnecessary work, but in dealing with precious metals the aim of the repairman should be to conserve the maximum amount of metal. Careless filing is sheer waste and the sign of a thoughtless workman.

The best way to proceed in learning to file is to form a clear mental picture of what you are trying to do and how you must go about doing it. Filing is the gradual reduction of metal to a desired size and shape, using the simplest of tools, the hand file. Many intricate shapes and designs can be developed by using the file alone. Interesting finishes can be given to metals with the file. Thus it can be seen that correct filing is of the utmost importance and should be studied in detail.

The usual procedure in filing and shaping tools or jewelry is first to rough out, with the coarse or rough files, the approximate size and shape. Proceed cautiously so that too much metal is not filed away in any one spot. When the work becomes close to the correct size and shape, change to finer files. As the job is completed, the finest files will leave a smooth surface.

To file a large piece of work, clamp it between the jaws of a vise attached to the workbench (see Fig. 2.12). Stand up to file. Hold the handle of the file (Fig. 2.13) in the right hand, the tip in the left. The right hand furnishes the push and power. The left hand guides the file and with a little pressure keeps it in constant contact with the metal being filed. With practice a straight filing stroke can be mastered. As the finer files are used, a lighter stroke is needed. In finishing the job a delicate touch or "feel" for the work comes into play and spells the difference between a superior and a mediocre job.

Roughing out should be done quickly. For speedy filing the answer is in method, not muscle. Remember to file away corners

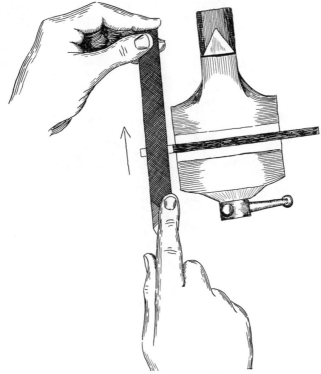

FIG. 2.12.   Using a file.

as soon as they are formed. The first few strokes will leave flat surfaces. The edges of the flat spots will be the corners to file away. As corners are filed away, flat spots again appear but also

FIG. 2.13.   File handle.

more corners. The corners present smaller cutting area, so the file will cut deeper and faster.

To finish the work, cross-filing and draw-filing can be used to advantage. After the work is rough-filed, select a finer file with closer teeth, and cross-file. In cross-filing, the strokes or lines are placed diagonally to those left by the rough file. Then more strokes or lines are placed perpendicular to these. In other words,

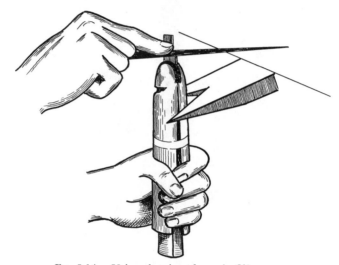

FIG. 2.14.   Using the ring clamp in filing.

two different sets of diagonal lines are placed over the rough cuts. Cross-filing removes all high spots remaining after rough-filing. Inspect the work, and it will be found that the first few strokes are cutting the high spots.

Draw-filing is done by using a small file, moving it across the work at right angles to the length of the file. This is more delicate filing, and there is more dependence on "touch" to maintain a square or flat surface. It is also possible to lay flat work on the file and rub back and forth until the desired flatness and finish are reached. The jewelry worker must do much filing that cannot be clamped in the bench vise. The student or beginner must learn to improvise and figure out various methods of holding work. The ring clamp with its leather padded jaws is useful for holding many articles (see Fig. 2.14). The ring clamp can be rested in the V slot of the bench pin and light filing and shaping satisfactorily executed. Simple squaring off of ends may be executed by holding the work in parallel pliers, resting the pliers in the V slot of the bench pin and filing at right angles to the slot in the pliers. The bench pin itself is a handy attachment for holding work for filing. Flat articles may be held with the fingers or a metal clamp, and light work with small files is easily done. When clamping work in the bench vise, it is best to line the jaws with copper to prevent marring the work.

Selecting the proper file depends on the nature of the work to be done. Jewelers should have on hand a wide selection of escapement files, and the larger regular files. They may be had in a variety of shapes, such as barrette, flat, half-round for the larger files and barrette, flat, half-round, oval, round, three-square, square, and knife-edge for the escapement files (see Fig. 1.15).

For successful roll-filing or pin-filing, hold the blank wire in a pin vise (see Fig. 2.15A). File a groove in the boxwood block as shown in Fig. 2.15B. The shaping of the groove is of utmost importance; it can be clearly seen from the drawing what will happen if the work is not properly shaped (see Fig. 2.15C). Remembering that files cut on the forward strokes, begin roll-filing by rolling the pin vise back and forth between the fingers. The rolls should be at least $1\frac{1}{2}$ turns in either direction. As the pin is rolled backward, the file is pushed forward. As the file is brought backward, the pin is rolled forward, and so back and forth until the pin is reduced to the desired size. The stroke backward does no cutting, so just enough pressure is needed to keep the pin in the groove. Finish the roll-filing by using a #4 file. One caution: Never stop the pin while the file is in motion because this will cause a flat side and spoil the job.

For maximum efficiency files must be kept sharp. Nothing is worse than to throw them together in the lap drawer where they will rub together and dull themselves. Many tools are kept conveniently in the lap drawer, but they should be tools that will not be damaged by contact with other tools. It is well to use a system of file arrangement, placing files in a rack or in slots apart from one another. The workman can best work out his own arrangement.

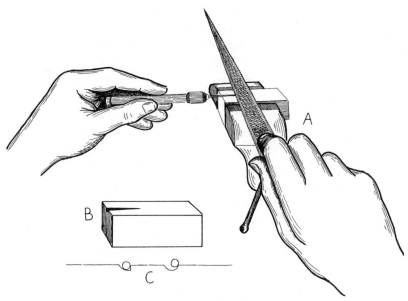

FIG. 2.15.   Roll-filing: *A,* using the pin vise; *B,* boxwood block with groove; *C,* proper and improper shape of groove.

Chapter 3

Soldering

Solders and fluxes
Melting ranges
Introduction to soldering
Hard-soldering by flame
Hard-soldering using the electric machine
Hard-soldering with the blowpipe
Soft-soldering
Exercises in hard-soldering

Solders and Fluxes

Using the correct solder is of prime importance and it must be kept in mind to match the solder with the article. If the article is stamped 10K use 10-karat solder; with 14K, 14-karat solder; with 18K, 18-karat solder, etc.

Platinum solder is available in different melting points as listed at the end of this section under Melting Ranges.

Low-karat gold solder is used when a low melting point is needed. This often occurs when soldering close to a previous solder joint. The low-karat solder will flow before the melting point of the solder holding the other joint is reached.

Silver solder can be bought as *regular, easy-flowing,* and *extra-easy-flowing.*

The solders mentioned are considered hard solders and will generally cover the needs of the average jewelry repairman. Special solders may be found by consulting material catalogs.

49

A good solder is valueless without a good flux. Be sure of your flux, and soldering, hard or soft, will come easily. Flux is used to prevent oxidization as the metal is heated. Without flux, a scale called oxide would form over the surfaces and prevent the solder from flowing. When applied, flux forms a coating that prevents oxidization.

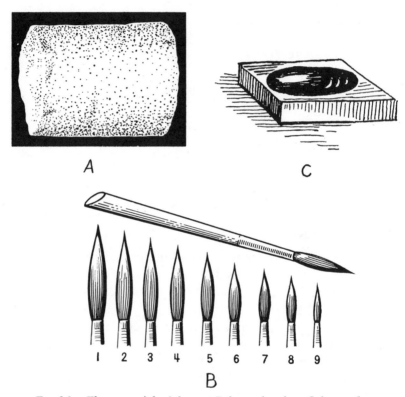

FIG. 3.1.   Flux material: *A*, borax; *B*, borax brushes; *C*, borax slate.

There are many fluxes on the market, most of them good. A poor flux can easily be recognized, and it is useless to continue using it after trying a few joints. Simply discard it. Find a good flux and stick with it.

A simple flux can be made of a thick paste of plain borax and water. This flux will bubble considerably while heating and will sometimes toss the solder away, but it is nevertheless a good flux and excellent results can be gotten with it (see Fig. 3.1A, B, C).

If there is trouble about obtaining a good joint, the reason will usually be found in improper fluxing, heating incorrectly, or failure to clean the joint. Oxidization on metal that takes place during hard-soldering may be removed in the pickle solution.

Melting Ranges

The lower temperature in the melting range of an alloy represents the temperature at which it begins to melt, and is called the "melting point." The higher temperature is the point at which the alloy is completely fluid, and is called the "flow point." Between these two temperatures, alloys have a mushy or semi-fluid structure, and will break under slight stress.

GOLD SOLDERS*

	Yellow	White	Green	Pink
For 18K work	1346-1436° F	1256-1346° F	1373-1436° F	1481-1499° F
For 14K work	1274-1418° F	1211-1364° F	1337-1398° F	1400-1490° F
For 10K work	1373-1391° F	1247-1346° F	1375-1396° F	1472-1499° F
For 8K work	1213-1413° F	1202-1294° F		1355-1382° F
For LOW work	1265-1283° F	1220-1247° F		1364-1401° F
Hard, 20		1526-1616° F		
Medium, 18		1292-1364° F		
All Purpose	1202-1229° F			

PLATINUM SOLDERS*

1000° (Extra Soft)	1400 (Extra Hard)
1100° (Soft)	1500 (Welding)
1200° (Medium)	1600 (Spec. Welding)
1300° (Hard)	Pure Platinum for Welding

Introduction to Soldering

In learning to do jewelry repairing, the most important operation for the beginner is soldering. Any other relative skill (filing,

* These tables are supplied by Hoover & Strong, Inc.

shaping, sawing, polishing, refinishing) is of little value without the ability to solder with confidence. And, since this operation is of such importance, it is well to concentrate on the skill of soldering as a separate subject having no relation to these other skills.

MELTING POINTS OF METALS (°F)

Tin	450
Bismuth	520
Cadmium	610
Lead	620
Zinc	780
Brass (copper 65%, zinc 35%)	930
Antimony	1165
Aluminum	1218
Silver (coin)	1615
Silver (sterling)	1640
Silver (fine)	1761
Gold	1945
Copper	2000
Brass (casting)	2075
Iron	2800
Palladium	2820
Platinum	3200
Iridium	4170
Carbon	6500

Consider what the beginner must eventually cope with in soldering as he advances and becomes adept at the craft of jewelry repairing. He must know how to solder with the various grades of solder, each one requiring a different heat; he must know how to control solder at one joint as he avoids melting the solder at a nearby joint; he must know how to mend and solder a broken section of metal that is surrounded by a series of soldered joints; and he must learn to do these jobs as though they were no problem. Obviously, the only way to attain this level of proficiency is through correct study and continued practice. Knowledge of metals and solders gained through experience will make a competent jewelry repairman.

With this in mind, the beginner should not attempt to rush into soldering on the precious metals. He certainly should not try to gain experience by experimenting on customer work brought into the store for repair. This practice can be costly, not only in damage to the article but also because a reputation is at stake every time a jewelry article is brought in for repair.

The best investment a beginner can make is in time—time enough to learn soldering on non-precious metals such as brass, copper, or nickel. Hours should be spent learning to work successfully with these metals and noting the minor differences in them as they respond to the soldering operation. Then, when one is ready for the precious metals, the minor differences encountered should not present a problem.

MELTING POINTS OF GOLD BY KARATS (°F)

Gold	1945
18K green	1810
18K red	1655
18K white	1730
18K yellow	1700
14K green	1765
14K red	1715
14K white	1825
14K yellow	1615
10K green	1580
10K red	1760
10K white	1975
10K yellow	1665

The beginner should acquaint himself thoroughly with the two methods of soldering: soldering using the torch and soldering with the electric soldering machine. He should allow himself time to develop skill in using both methods. Even though the methods may be partially understood, it would be an advantage to review the techniques of the two methods and to look carefully for bits of information that will round out one's knowledge or fill in important gaps.

Hard-soldering by Flame (Oxygen-Gas)

It has been the writer's experience to note that in the larger cities the jewelry-repair shops are usually equipped with a torch soldering outfit (as well as an electric soldering machine, in some instances), while in the smaller towns the electric machine seems to be more prevalent. This is not primarily due to a preference in the soldering, but rather to the lack of natural-gas service. Hence, the electric soldering machine is a real convenience.

Thanks to the excellent service being rendered by distributors of manufactured gas, many jewelers in isolated localities are availing themselves of the advantage of flame-soldering. The tanks of gas are installed and replaced in the same manner as tanks of oxygen. The tanks are delivered to the door of the jeweler, thus enabling him to offer all the services of the jeweler located in a larger city.

With an adequate torch outfit the jewelry repairman is not limited in the least on any soldering job. There are many very intricate soldering jobs that, while not impossible with the machine, require a specialist's skill to perform. The average jewelry repairman does not place himself in the category of specialist and might very easily decide to use the torch exclusively rather than the machine. While this book does not recommend one method over the over, it does endeavor to emphasize the advantages of both mediums.

If a jeweler decides to install a flame-soldering outfit, then the most sensible thing to do is to purchase the most versatile apparatus, regardless of cost. Cost is a negligible factor in so important a decision. The best in torch equipment will last a lifetime; upkeep and repair are also negligible.

The average torch outfit includes an oxygen guage and a torch with four or five different sized nozzles. The torch has two hose

connections, one for oxygen and one for gas (natural or manufactured). Each hose has an adjustment to regulate the flow of gas
and of oxygen. By adjusting the oxygen and gas regulators, the
desired flame intensity is reached. This will remain constant
throughout the soldering operation.

Depending on the nature of the work, a large brush-type flame
or a fine pinpoint flame may be desirable. See Fig. 3.2. To make

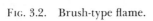

Fig. 3.2.   Brush-type flame.

a broad brush flame, attach the largest nozzle to the tip of the
torch. Turn on the gas only and ignite. Add just enough oxygen
to produce a broad blue flame. This flame is good for a number
of jobs that do not require intense concentration or a quick flow
of solder, for example, soldering band rings.

When the torch is first lighted (without the addition of oxygen)
the flame will appear to be yellow in color. As oxygen is introduced
to the gas, the yellow color gradually fades and the flame becomes
bluish. This is an average flame for average soldering. A yellow
flame does not have sufficient intensity to flow hard solder. The
yellow color must be eliminated by the addition of oxygen as the
flame becomes blue.

Depending on the size of the article to be soldered, a large,
medium, or small nozzle may be used on the torch head. Frequently more heat than is generated by the average blue flame is
required to complete the soldering operation. This may be due
to the weight of the shank (if it is a ring-sizing job) or the weight
of the article (if it is a jewelry piece).

To increase the intensity, turn the gas regulator to maximum
or near maximum flow and add just enough oxygen for the flame
not to be blown out (too much oxygen will extinguish the flame).
This will concentrate the flame, bringing it to a fine pinpoint.

The addition of oxygen will always change the brush appearance of the flame to a fine, narrow, pointed type of flame.

The range of heat possible with only one nozzle can now be understood and to apply this flexibility to five nozzles of different hole diameters widens the range of heat even more. Suffice it to say that the jeweler's torch outfit will accommodate any soldering problem that may arise.

As compared to soldering with the electric soldering machine, the flame will leave a wider area of discoloration. Due to the speed in which solder flows, using the machine, the discoloration spread does not get very far from the joint. This is neither a handicap nor a particular advantage since both methods use the pickle solution to remove oxidization and flux scale. There is no effort on the part of the operator—the solution does the work. Of course, there may be rare jobs that may indicate a quick solder is more desirable, and it is well to be conscious of this unique feature that only the electric machine provides. As opposed to this feature, there will be many jobs that demand a slower heat that is provided only by the flame. For this reason, it cannot be said that one method is superior to the other, and should be used exclusively over the other. There is a place for both methods, and though it may develop that one method is preferred over the other (due to personal preference or adaptability), both methods should be used for their advantages when the opportunity arises.

The formula for mixing the pickle solution will be found in Chapter 16, Solutions and Formulae. The features for correct handling and mixing should be carefully observed. Should an accident occur during the mixing of the solution, it is well to have a quantity of ordinary baking soda within easy reach. The baking soda will neutralize acid spilled on hands or clothing.

No ring with a stone or enamel should be thrown into the pickle solution while hot. To do so may cause cracks to form. When the ring has cooled, it may be placed in the cold pickle solution with no danger to most stones. Porous stones, such as the opal, onyx, sardonyx, and turquoise, should not be placed in a hot pickle solution.

Hard-soldering Using the Electric Machine

The normal function of the electric soldering machine is to solder a joint in seconds. The heat indicator should be set as close as possible to what the operator thinks is the correct adjustment; then, the contact is made. If the solder does not flow immediately, the heat indicator is usually set too low for the object. It could very well be that the heat is set too high and, although the risk of burning the joint is great, it is possible for the quick, intense heat to oxidize the joint, rendering the solder useless and thereby destroying the contact altogether.

With a clean joint carefully fluxed and with the rheostat set exactly right, the contact will be positive and immediate, causing an almost instant flow of solder. Therefore, the most important feature appears to be the technique of the operator in synchronizing his skill with the capabilities of the machine. The machine will respond according to the skill of the operator.

One who has used a flame exclusively might well find the machine a disappointing medium for soldering. By the same token, those who are experts with the electric machine often find the torch method exasperating, for they are accustomed to more speed in soldering than the torch will produce.

The speed of soldering a joint is a negligible factor—the soldering operation is only one of many. But, since the timing of the flow of solder is so different in changing from one method to the other, the operator is likely to attach more importance to it than it warrants. It is far better to be versatile and accept the advantages of both methods of soldering.

To continue with the electric machine, the most important feature of all is cleanliness—cleanliness of joint and cleanliness of carbon. If these two conditions exist, chances are almost perfect since the only other factor is heat regulation (assuming that a good grade of flux is being used).

After many joints have been soldered on the carbon, the point of contact should be carefully cleaned by using an old file to remove hard scale. Each soldering operation will leave a slight scale of old flux on the carbon and if these are not removed, the surface will soon be covered with the scaly substance making it impossible to achieve a clean connection or contact.

If the solder will not flow, after attempting to solder a joint, one should begin again from scratch. This means to clean the carbon and also the surfaces of the joint to be soldered, in addition to applying fresh flux. Possibly a readjustment is indicated in the heat regulation. Failure to obtain a joint will always have a logical reason. Mechanical failure in the machine should not be overlooked. A good test for this is to set the rheostat in the center and touch the carbon with the clamp attachment. Sparks should be seen immediately. If sparks (electric arcs) are seen, the reason for the trouble will more than likely be the operator (assuming that a quality flux is being used).

To reduce the occasional pit-holes that form at the point of contact, observe two controlling factors. Do not press excessively during the operation and do not lift the work away from the carbon as soon as solder is seen to flow. The first reaction should be to release the foot contact. Then lift the work away from the carbon. If an excessive amount of pit-holes or marred surfaces result, the reason is probably too much heat. This condition will cause the metal to melt or become nearly fluid. All that is desired is that the solder flows and this does not require the amount of heat sufficient to melt the article being soldered.

Many soldering machines are equipped with a carbon pencil. To use this, attach the soldering tweezers (attached to the machine) to the article, hold the article in the bench vise, and with the point of the carbon, heat the article at the spot to be soldered.

The most-used carbon attachment is the round, tapered carbon, which has many uses, the most important being ring soldering. This phase of soldering is dealt with in detail in Chapter 6, Ring Sizing (see Fig. 6.7D).

Another useful carbon shape is the square-cornered carbon with an inclined face presenting a sharp edge (see Fig. 9.4). This may be used for chain soldering, spectacle-frame soldering, repairing prongs on ring mountings, and many other jobs.

Various machine clamps are used to hold articles while solder-ing. The clamp selected will depend on the size and shape of the article and the primary duty of the clamp, which is to complete the circuit when the carbon is contacted.

Hard-soldering with the Blowpipe

Many beginners have a great deal of trouble using the blow-pipe (Fig. 3.3) correctly. What is wanted from the blowpipe is a

FIG. 3.3.   Blowpipe.

steady, continuous blue flame that will solder any article. How to get it? First fill the cheeks with air (see Fig. 3.4). Close the passage leading to the throat and with the cheeks still full of air breathe through the nose. With the blowpipe in the mouth, the amount of air forced through it can be controlled by the cheeks. As air is released through the blowpipe, additional air is breathed through the nose into the lungs. With the lungs filled, the air is allowed to enter the cheeks by opening the passage in the throat. The cheeks never become empty, and a steady pressure is obtained. If this is properly executed, the operator will not get out of breath and in fact can continue the blowing for quite some time.

To gain experience with the blowpipe the same procedures may be followed as explained above, Hard-soldering by Flame.

In Summary

1. Be sure all joints to be soldered are absolutely clean. In pre-paring joints the contact surfaces should be lightly filed to insure absence of oxidation or dirt.
2. Do not use excessive heat. It is better to stay on the low side.
3. Do not press hard. This will mar the metal.

4. Have the hands well braced during the soldering operation. The article must be held firm and still.
5. Release contact the instant solder flows by lifting the foot.
6. Lift the article from the carbon only after the current is off.
7. If there is trouble securing a connection on the carbon, move the contact point to another position on the carbon. If results are negative, the fault generally lies with the joint on the article. Check it for cleanliness, remove the old flux, and then try again. If there is still trouble in getting a connection, wash the carbon with a wet cloth, soldering the joint while the carbon is still damp.

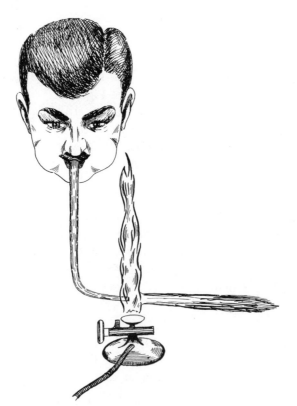

FIG. 3.4.   Using the blowpipe.

8. With every soldering machine there is or should be a folder of instructions on how to get good results with that particular machine. Study these carefully and if any trouble in soldering arises, write to the company that made the machine. The manufacturer should be able to tell you exactly what your trouble is.

Soft-soldering

Soft-soldering procedures are much the same as those in hard-soldering. A different solder and flux is used with a very low degree of heat.

For flame-soldering, clean and flux the joints, apply a small amount of soft solder. Direct an alcohol flame to the joint and slowly build up the heat until the solder flows.

For practice work, solder two pieces of silver or brass wire together flowing the solder first on one of the edges of the joint, then on the other. Place them together over the flame and allow the solder to flow together. Do not put soft-soldered joints in a pickle solution.

For machine-soldering, use a low degree of heat and remember that it is not necessary to have the point of contact exactly at the spot you wish the solder to flow. It is only necessary to build up enough heat around the area to melt the solder. Allow the heated article, not the carbon, to melt the solder. The carbon will heat the article, causing the article to heat the solder and thus starting it to flow.

Exercises in Hard-soldering

Before the beginner can qualify to work with the precious metals he should complete the following exercises (or the equivalent).

Exercise 1

Using common wire, brass or nickel (available from all supply houses in assorted diameters), cut off sections long enough to make rings of approximately size 7 (in the smaller diameters), and size 10 (in the larger wires). (See Fig. 3.5.) The rings may be rounded by lightly pounding them on the ungrooved steel mandrel. Make up an assortment of rings using all available diameters.

In this practice work we are concerned primarily with the soldering operation, although a secondary function must be performed as flawlessly as possible in order to insure complete success in soldering. This is the preparation of the joint, or the filing operation. All joints must be square or flush in soldering of this nature, therefore great care is indicated to file and bring the joint together as shown in Fig. 3.5. The surfaces around the joint are lightly roughed up (in reality a cleaning operation) so that the solder will adhere more readily to the metal surface. This is done by lightly rubbing a small jeweler's file over the area. When the joint is flush, the flux may be applied sparingly using a camel's-

FIG. 3.5.   Flush, clean joint.

hair brush, being sure that it runs through the joint. How much solder to use? This will, of course depend on the thickness of the wire. Since there is no need to use more solder than is necessary (the excess must be removed), be conservative. Small bits of solder may be cut off from the sheet of silver solder. These fragments may be picked up by the tip of the moist camel's-hair brush and placed directly over the joint (which has already been fluxed). In cutting these fragments of solder, one should estimate the probable size needed for the work at hand. For example, as larger rings are soldered, the size of the solder fragments should be increased.

The first method of soldering will be to clamp the ring on the asbestos or charcoal block using small U-shaped sections of binding wire. (See Fig. 3.6.) Apply the flame first to the bare area near the joint, gradually moving it back and forth, to the joint and away, warming up the entire area. Soon the heat will increase at the joint as the motion of the flame becomes more steady. When the melting point of the solder is reached, it will flow quickly into the joint; then, the flame is removed. This operation illustrates

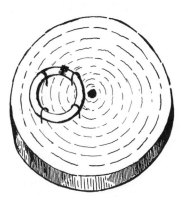

FIG. 3.6. Clamping ring to asbestos soldering pad.

how articles may be pinned to the soldering block, and it provides experience in soldering on the block as opposed to soldering articles by holding them in tweezers. This is not a waste of time for the technique of soldering on the block is quite different from soldering articles suspended in air (held with the tweezers). The soldering block will hold a more intense heat, and for a longer period of time—two points worth remembering when using the asbestos or the charcoal block.

In Fig. 3.7, the same operation is performed using the soldering

FIG. 3.7.   Holding ring with tweezers.

tweezers. This is the more practical way to do this type of ring sizing since the article can be plunged immediately into the pickle solution to remove the discoloration caused by heat. This method also affords an easy approach to the joint as well as better control of the solder. First, the ring should be warmed up gradually in order to dry out the flux and hold the solder; then, the heat is increased as the flame is waved back and forth in ever-shortening arcs. Soon, the melting point of the solder is reached as it disappears into the joint.

In Fig. 6.7, we see the same ring, fluxed, with solder applied, and in position against the carbon of the electric soldering machine. This method of soldering will be much quicker than either of the methods just discussed. The difficulty, if any, will be in finding the correct machine adjustment suitable for the weight of the ring. These machines have rheostats that will locate the adjustments exactly, and it is a matter of the operator's learning how to get the best performance from the machine. Until the correct adjustment is found for a given weight, the shank may be burned or melted (if the heat is set too high) or the solder will dry out and become useless (creating a scale that prevents the solder from flowing) if the adjustment is too low. If the adjustment is set too low, when the electrical contact is made, the solder fails to reach flowing heat, or if it does it is too late to flow (meaning that the flux has been rendered useless prior to the moment of solder flow). In some cases the solder will flow and form a ball, but will not flow into the joint. This predicament cannot be successfully corrected simply by applying more flux. In most instances, old flux must be removed, the joint cleaned thoroughly, and the soldering operation begun again—with fresh flux and fresh solder. Of course, the heat indicator on the rheostat should be raised slightly.

Exercise 2

To gain experience in more complicated soldering, use the same rings to make repeated solder joints—new joints. This will entail sawing through at a different location each time until the individual ring is used up. The complications will become obvious, for as the shank becomes filled with solder joints there is constant danger of loosening previous joints or otherwise disturbing them. It should be interesting for the beginner to see how many different joints he can make in a practice ring shank without disturbing the others. Since silver solder may be obtained as *regular,* *easy-flowing,* and *extra-easy-flowing,* it would indeed be good practice to become acquainted with the differences in melting points. The advantage of using *easy-flowing* solder near a joint that was soldered with *regular* flowing solder will be obvious at the first attempt to solder such a joint, since the *easy-flowing* solder will flow and secure the new joint before the melting point of the *regular* flowing solder is reached. Needless to say, all the thicknesses of wire should be worked with, from the smallest to the largest. Only in this way can the beginner become adept at evaluating heats and solders as related to metal thickness.

During the soldering of rings containing multiple joints, the advantages of using the charcoal or asbestos block become apparent. If it is suspected that a nearby joint will become unsoldered or shift its position, the situation can be brought under control by pinning the ring firmly to the block before soldering the new joint. On a level surface, if the ring is pinned firmly to the block, the new joint may be soldered without experiencing any shift from neighboring joints, even though the solder of the neighboring joints may become fluid.

Exercise 3

Still using the brass or nickel wire, try soldering straight sections or lengths together, but using different diameters or weights of wire. They may be soldered in either pattern: end-to-end or in T-formations. This type of practice work is more easily handled using the soldering block or the electric soldering machine.

To use the soldering block, first pin the sections firmly in the desired position (end-to-end or T-formation). The problems to overcome are these: making the solder joint without allowing the heat to cause a shift in position, thus spoiling the joint; getting the solder to flow equally on each section (there will be a tendency for the solder to flow on the lighter section first unless the flame is directed more steadily on the larger section; actually, the heavier piece is simply favored more in heat exposure as the flame is waved back and forth over the area); making a solder joint without melting the lighter section, when using a very thin wire. All of these operations will teach the beginner the importance of evaluating the weight of the metals to be soldered.

To complete this exercise, try soldering light wire to heavy wire, but in two places as seen in Fig. 3.8. The two joints can be soldered simultaneously if pinned on the soldering block; it will be two individual operations using the electric soldering machine.

Exercise 4

Frequently, it will be advantageous to "sweat" a joint; that is, flowing solder first in one section, then on the other, and bringing the two sections in contact *after* solder has been flowed on the surfaces to be joined. (See Fig. 3.9.) By heating the heavier section

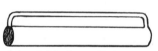
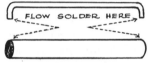

FIG. 3.8. Soldering a light wire to a heavy wire.   FIG. 3.9. "Sweating" two wire joints.

to the melting point of the solder, the "sweating" action is accomplished. This method may be demonstrated even more clearly in Fig. 3.10. Here we see two sections of flat brass stock, accurately filed and finished to precisely matching proportions. The thicknesses illustrated may be 1.5 mm each. Our problem will be to

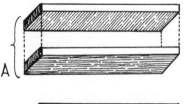

A

B

FIG. 3.10. "Sweating" two sections of flat brass stock.

solder these two pieces together in perfectly matched positions so that the result will be one section of flat brass stock measuring 3 mm in thickness. A successful "sweating" job will bring the two pieces together flush, without lines, bubbles in the solder, or other imperfections. To do this, lay both pieces on the soldering block; flux the areas well; apply a minimum of solder, just enough to cover the entire surface. Apply the heat of the flame very slowly and evenly so that when the melting point of the solder is reached it will "flood" the surface at once. The result will be an even film of solder without ridges or irregularities. Clean the two sections and re-flux. Place one section over the other, and without the addition of more solder, apply the gradual heat of the flame, taking care to control the evenness of heat throughout the length of the two sections. Have a pair of tweezers (or a length of wire) ready to nudge the top section in position as it is sweated to the lower section. Even with the aid of binding wire the two pieces may settle together in an out-of-flush condition, and since the alignment error will be very slight it may be nudged into perfect alignment as the solder sets and hardens. The sides of the two sweated sections may be rubbed over emery paper, #1 or #0, and examined for flaws.

Exercise 5

The final exercise in soldering should be devoted to the soldering of various thicknesses of wire to larger sections of flat stock (this of varying thickness). See Fig. 3.11. This is a fairly heavy piece of brass stock (about 1.5 mm thick) to which is soldered two pieces of brass wire (four solders in all). Other designs may be imagined to give one an objective in gaining soldering experience. See Fig. 3.12. Using this idea, try soldering wire to thinner and thinner plates, to the point where there is risk of melting the

FIG. 3.11. Soldering four joints on one bar.

FIG. 3.12. Working with multiple solder joints.

plate. (These thin plates may be rolled out to suitable thickness if one has access to a rolling mill; otherwise it will be necessary to use whatever is at hand in scrap metal.) When working with the various shapes and widths of flat stock and wire, it may be necessary to solder some joints in the conventional manner and sweat others. Whatever the method, this will complete the background needed to proceed with work on precious metals.

Chapter 4

Cleaning Jewelry

Hand cleaning
Ultrasonic cleaning
Steam cleaning
Summary of cleaning procedures

TODAY, with all the equipment now available to the jeweler, cleaning jewelry is not the problem it once was, but it is well to understand the nature of the degrees of contamination as well as the specific action needed to bring about the desired result in the shortest possible time.

In restoring a piece of jewelry, the normal contaminants are grease and dirt, under which we find tarnish in varying degrees. The grease and dirt may be composed of an unlimited number of ingredients such as skin oils, cosmetic creams, powder, hand lotions, soap, and muffin mix, all liberally blended with common yard dirt. The removal of this coating should be viewed as the primary objective, separate from the refinishing operation. In fact, any attempts to remove tarnish is useless until this coating is removed and though an ultrasonic cleaning machine may do both, it nevertheless removes the grime before the vibrations can go to work on the tarnish.

Hand Cleaning

For those who do not have an ultrasonic cleaning machine, it is necessary to remove the grime by using a stock solution (see

Stock Solution #1 in Chapter 16, Solutions and Formulae). After soaking in the solution, articles are hand scrubbed. The solution may be used cold or warm, and in stubborn cases articles may be boiled in a covered pan.

Another popular but very powerful solution is Stock Solution #2 (see Chapter 16, Solutions and Formulae). After noting the ingredients and the warning, the solution is obviously reserved for severely contaminated articles, including corroded ones. Best results are obtained when the articles are allowed to soak for at least 5 minutes, longer if necessary.

These two solutions are all that is needed for normal hand cleaning methods. They are usually stored in glass jugs containing one gallon. Solution #1 will lose strength after it is poured from the jug and may be revitalized from time to time by adding small amounts of 27-28 per cent aqua-ammonia. Solution #2 is used less and rarely needs revitalizing other than to add more solution to the container as it is depleted by use.

Cyanide is a very valuable aid in the restoration of jewelry surfaces and, though it will be discussed in this chapter, it is not a cleaning agent. The cyanide dip is part of the process of cleaning, yet it does one job only—the removal of tarnish. Neither is cyanide an acid. The jewelry repairman should be perfectly clear about the limitations of cyanide and not use it for any task other than the removal of tarnish. Cyanide should be kept in a tight glass container, out of the reach of children, and be plainly marked: **CYANIDE, DEADLY POISON.** During the cyanide dip, jewelry may be suspended from long brass or copper wires, eliminating the need to expose the hands to the solution. When removed from the cyanide dip, the articles are rinsed under running water, dipped in alcohol, and placed in sawdust to dry.

In hand-washing jewelry, the conventional bone-handle washout brush has been used for decades due to its construction. The bristles are attached with stainless steel wire that resists the strongest solutions. Also available are the new nylon-bristle washout brushes. Small toothbrushes may be used to good advantage particularly for such areas as the inside of rings and underneath stones.

Ultrasonic Cleaning

Ultrasonic cleaning machines come closer to performing all cleaning chores in the repair department than any medium of cleaning ever presented to the trade. For example, customers' rings may be dropped into the tank while they are in the store. The rings may be handed to them in less than five minutes time with contamination and tarnish gone. In addition, the jewelry will be bright as though it had been slightly polished.

In the shop, articles should be ultrasonically cleaned before performing any work on them. This prevents unwanted discoloration during soldering procedures. After polishing, the repaired articles should be ultrasonically cleaned again to remove tripoli and rouge. (These two abrasives have always presented a removal problem to jewelers through the ages; ultrasonics can remove abrasive contamination in a minute or two depending on the degree.) If additional handling is necessary after the removal of rouge and tripoli, the article may again be ultrasonically cleaned for a few seconds to remove finger prints or invisible smudges that could later cause tarnish. After ultrasonic cleaning, articles should be wrapped untouched in tissue.

The manufacturers of ultrasonic cleaning machines have solutions compounded especially for their machines. It is suggested that instructions accompanying the machines be followed closely and that the recommended solutions be used. Experimentation with "private mixtures" could damage the tank.

Although ultrasonic vibrations will attack and remove all contaminants such as cosmetics, dough, skin oils, dirt, and grease, the greatest challenge to the machine is the removal of the packed contamination found behind stones of ladies rings. Actually, this contamination is a combination of all the ingredients mentioned above, and the machines will remove it, given time (and presoaking). The packed grime found behind these stones (underneath the mounting) should first be loosened or otherwise broken up using a fine pointed instrument. After all, why not conserve the machine by allowing the solutions and vibrations to get at the contamination and work faster. Then, too, some articles are so heavily tarnished that the machine takes longer than is necessary to remove it. Conserve the machine and use cyanide, which removes tarnish in seconds.

All things considered, ultrasonics will perform a large percentage of the cleaning operations without manual assistance. It is considered a necessity in the jewelry store of today.

Steam Cleaning

Another important piece of equipment in the jewelry cleaning department is the steam cleaner, a luxury seen mainly in stores doing a volume of jewelry repair. Using live steam for blasting out the contamination collecting in crevices, and particularly behind stones in rings, pins, or brooches, has been common in the jewelry field for decades and will probably continue so in spite of the advent of ultrasonics. However, a steam cleaner should not be purchased as a substitute for ultrasonics because the two mediums cannot be evaluated in that way. A steam cleaner is purchased for its peculiar advantage, and an ultrasonic machine is purchased to obtain advantages of a different nature. They do not conflict but rather complement each other especially when they are available for use in the same repair shop.

Articles are held in tweezers and placed under the steam jet, twisting and turning so that all surfaces are exposed to the live steam. The operation usually takes a few seconds.

Summary of Cleaning Procedures

1. Before cleaning any jewelry, see that all stones are secure. Tighten any loose stones.

2. Remove all dirt, grease or foreign matter by way of hand cleaning or using ultrasonic machine.

3. Dip in cyanide for thirty seconds to one minute, depending on how badly the jewelry is oxidized.

4. Rinse in running water and dry.

5. Polish the work lightly, using the cloth rouge buff. This is usually all that is necessary to restore a bright luster.

6. Wash again in the cleaning solution or ultrasonic machine.

7. Dip in alcohol.

8. Dry in sawdust.

Chapter 5

Buffing and Polishing

IF ANYONE could say that one operation is more important than another in the shaping and finishing of jewelry, the choice would probably be the buffing and polishing operation, no doubt because the final appearance of all jewelry governs its acceptability to the customer. And too, this operation enhances all the other operations and would naturally be of prime importance.

Polishing motors or dust collectors, as they are commonly called, should be of adequate strength (at least ¼ horsepower) and one equipped with two speeds will have an advantage over a single-speed motor. The speeds are usually 1725 rpm and 3450 rpm. Some compact machines have only one tapered spindle, requiring a change from rouge to tripoli buffs during a polishing operation. A machine with two tapered spindles, one side using rouge and the other tripoli, will naturally save time by eliminating the necessity for changing buffs too frequently. Metal guards are fitted over the spindles or buffing arbors and, with the suction apparatus directly beneath the spindle, the dust from rouge and tripoli is collected to be sent to the refiners when the bag becomes full. Over a period of time the accumulated dust will yield enough gold to be considered a worthwhile asset to the repair department.

Tripoli and rouge are the polishing agents most often used with the jewelers' polishing lathe. Tripoli brushes and buffs are usually kept in a drawer under the left spindle where all the tripoli buffing is done. The rouge buffs and brushes are kept in the right drawer beneath the rouge spindle. The rouge and tripoli buffs are *never* kept in the same drawers for fear of contamination—there is no better word, for a rouge buff or brush will become contaminated with even a small amount of tripoli. This contamination will show up in the next rouge buffing operation. Instead of the usual mirror finish there will be a dullness or satiny finish that will not disappear until a perfectly clean rouge buff is used. In order to keep the rouge buffs from becoming contaminated (even when the buffs are never mixed) always wipe the article after using the tripoli abrasive. It is possible to "carry over" the tripoli on the article to the rouge buff. Although this "carry over" may be infinitesimal, the cumulative effect of it can ruin a rouge buff.

Tripoli may be obtained in brick form or in peel-back containers to protect the fingers. Tripoli has the faculty of imbedding itself in the skin of the fingers. Rouge may be obtained in raw stick form or in peel-back containers and is equally as hard to remove from the fingers as tripoli. Although most tripoli contains essentially the same ingredients (an abrasive with oil), rouge may be purchased in a variety of forms and colors, the red product being the most common. There is also yellow rouge, black rouge, and white rouge; each one is intended to produce a special finish on certain metals. Their consistency will range from the very dry to medium oily. The purposes of the various rouges may be learned by studying suppliers' catalogs where the products are pictured and described.

When using tripoli it will be found to be a fast-cutting abrasive that will remove minor scratches or file marks left from previous operations. It will smooth out all surfaces but it will not bright polish. Obviously, the better prepared the work is before presenting it to the tripoli buff, the less time is spent using the tripoli, and the smoother the end result will be.

When using the rouge buff, the cutting action is almost nil and may be better described as a part burnishing, part polishing action depending on the applied pressure. Rouge should be applied to the buff very sparingly for an excess of some rouges may result in a slight satin finish similar to the tripoli result. If a buff becomes "loaded" with too much rouge, some of it can be removed by pressing the exposed wood of an emery stick to the spinning buff, thus wearing it off.

After buffing any article, it should be cleaned thoroughly in the cleaning solution to remove all traces of polishing agents. The article is then dipped in alcohol and dried in sawdust.

For an average shop the following wheels and buffs should be available to the repairman: emery inside ring buffs, felt inside ring buffs, felt combination wheel and inside ring buffs, bristle wheel brushes, steel bristle wheel brushes, brass wheel brushes, muslin wheel buffs, cotton flannel wheel buffs, and optional odd shapes for special buffing operations.

Emery ring buffs (Fig. 5.1) are available from any supply house

FIG. 5.1.   Emery inside ring buffs.

and are great timesavers as well as excellent finishing mediums. The average assortment of emery ring buffs includes a wood taper and may be made of paper or cloth. Of course, the cloth product will be more durable (and more expensive) having the additional advantage of resisting tears common to the paper variety. They are also available in specific grits (by the dozen) and it is perhaps more economical to purchase the most used grits in quantity rather than by assortment. The main advantage of the emery buff is to

speed up a portion of the rough filing work preparatory to polishing.

A combination inside ring buff (Fig. 5.2) saves time by elimi-

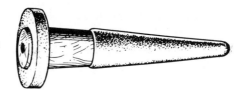

Fig. 5.2. A combination felt
ring and wheel buff.

nating a buff changing operation. It will accommodate all the surfaces the ring has to offer—inside, outside, and the sides. Its taper
is perfect for smoothing out the inside of the ring while the flat
surface of the wheel section is ideal for the outside surface. Also,
the sides of the wheel present an excellent plane to polish out the
file marks on the sides of the shank. Also available are tiny inside
ring buffs (without the combined wheel) which are used for children's and baby rings.

Bristle wheel brushes (Fig. 5.3) have many uses, ranging from

Fig. 5.3. Bristle wheel brush.

small pieces of jewelry (such as ring mounting and joint and pin
catches) to large pieces of silverware. The 3-inch bristle brushes
may be used on articles that have corners and crevices that cannot
be reached by the ordinary flat buff. They are used mainly for
buffing in and around ring mountings, etc. It is desirable to have
one for tripoli and one for rouge.

Brass wheel brushes are flexible and may be used for dull-finishing the softer metals while the steel wheel brushes are less flexible, and are more useful on the harder metals where a satin finish is desired.

Cotton-flannel wheel buffs (Fig. 5.4) are used for work of general nature. Two are necessary, one for tripoli and the other for rouge. These buffs are available by diameter dimension: 4-inch, 5-inch, and 6-inch, and perhaps other dimensions by special order. Care should be used particularly with the tripoli side for a buff

FIG. 5.4.   Cotton flannel wheel buff.

this large will be traveling at a greatly increased rate of speed which will allow the tripoli to cut into the metal much more quickly—and particularly if excessive pressure is exerted. After charging this buff with tripoli it is not necessary to apply more tripoli each time it is used. Rather, apply the tripoli when results indicate it is needed. The rouge side is not as critical although the buff should not become over-charged with rouge. This will tend to slow down the ultimate bright polish rather than hasten it.

Muslin wheel buffs (Fig. 5.5) represent the "elite" buffs, the handle-with-care buffs that must be thrown away or reduced in rank should they become contaminated by association with common buffs. These buffs are reserved for polishing silver surfaces that demand a high and flawless luster (some repairmen reserve them for special gold polishing as well). Even before using, this buff must be carefully examined for flaws (small knots or flubs in the fabric) which will surely be reflected in the highly sensitive surfaces of sterling silver. Rouge is applied sparingly but uniformly for uneven "loading" will be reflected as a spotty surface

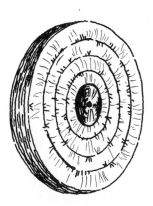

Fig. 5.5.   Muslin wheel buff.

polish. These buffs are available as stitched or unstitched (Fig. 5.6), the latter being used for large sterling surfaces as trays, bowls, etc. Since accuracy of buffing is so important these buffs are available with leather and/or lead centers which are carefully made true on the spindle thereby eliminating the possibility of a spotty,

Fig. 5.6.   Buffing a curved surface.

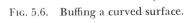

though polished surface that could result from using an out-of-true wheel buff. Silver polishing is an art by itself and though the metal may be less expensive than gold the finishing is far more critical and should be viewed with perhaps even more respect.

Solid felt wheel buffs (Fig. 5.7) are made of high-grade wool of

Fig. 5.7.   Solid felt wheel buff.

uniform texture and are most in demand when a hard, firm surface is wanted. This type of buff cuts rapidly with tripoli, as well as providing a quick polish when used with rouge.

A discussion of the polishing lathe should begin with a warning to respect its capability for inflicting serious personal injury as well as damage to many articles of jewelry. The spinning buffs have a tendency to snatch at anything coming in contact with them. The down draft created by the blower to the dust collector may cause an article of clothing, such as a tie, to fall into the wheel. Work should be held freely so that in the event the wheel snatches it away the fingers will not be damaged. Should an accident occur the best course to follow is to cut off the machine immediately. Begin now to train your mind to react accordingly.

Polishing procedure is as follows: assuming the article has been soldered, pickled, and filed, preparatory to buffing, and depending on the article, select a cloth buff, an inside ring buff, or a stiff bristle brush. Apply a little tripoli and remove all scratches remaining from the filing operation. When the tripoli buffing is complete, wipe or wash off the article before using the rouge buff. Be sure the article is dry before using the rouge buff. Final finishes are usually done with the rouge charged flannel buff since its higher speed (due to its larger diameter) provides a higher polish. When a brilliant finish is reached, wash the article in a heated cleaning solution. Dip in alcohol and dry in sawdust.

There are always articles that present polishing problems where the metal is too thin to apply pressure. These may be supported by a piece of wood and then presented to the buff (Fig. 5.8). After soldering chains there is always the problem of restoring the soldered area to match the rest of the chain. Fig. 5.9 shows a suggested way to prevent the chain from becoming entangled in the buff. By holding the chain around the ring clamp and the loose

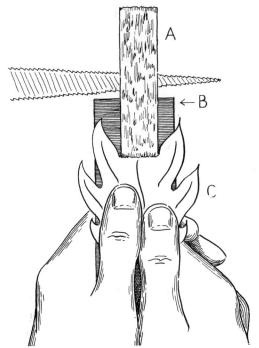

FIG. 5.8.   Supporting an article in polishing: *A*, polishing buff; *B*, support; *C*, article.

section away from the whirling buff, sections of the chain may be polished one at a time with little fear that it may become entangled in the buff. Of course, the chain is not allowed to become

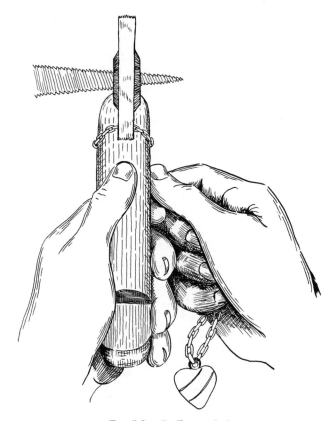

FIG. 5.9.   Buffing a chain.

slack on the ring clamp for this could conceivably cause an accident.

Fig. 5.10 shows how the bristle brush (in this case, not a black bristle brush but one of a softer bristle, usually of a light color) bends easily and fits into little corners and crevices.

Fig. 5.11 shows the ring buff in action. This is a combination felt wheel and inside ring buff. The three positions of buffing are shown accommodating all surfaces.

In buffing and polishing metal surfaces, it is important to re-

Fig. 5.10.   Buffing the back of a bar pin.

member that the final mirror finish may be attained by way of different methods or a combination of methods. For example, a ring may be sawed and filed out of raw stock and brought to a mirror finish by the file, tripoli and rouge method. It is also possible to prepare the ring for final polishing by using only the emery stick and cone method since they may be purchased in any number of grits ranging from the very coarse to the very fine.

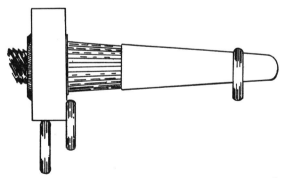

Fig. 5.11.   Polishing all ring surfaces using combination buff.

Without using a file the surface may be prepared suitably for the polishing motor. Coarse emery sticks take the place of files. Then, the finer emery sticks may be used, gradually changing to the finest grit. By this time there are no lines remaining for the surfaces have begun to assume a polished appearance similar to the appearance seen after using tripoli—not brilliant, but semibright. By skipping the use of tripoli, we have a minor advantage. The surfaces are dry with no abrasive carry-over. A few light touches to the rouge wheel buff will complete the brilliant polished appearance desired.

Of course, the emery stick may be used on the side surfaces of the ring as well as the outer surface. The only problem would be the inside surfaces, but a little ingenuity can solve this problem. By wrapping emery paper (or cloth) about a round wooden stick, the inside surfaces may be easily reached. Of course, the emery ring cones or shells will accomplish the same result but it is well to know how to do these things by hand at the jeweler's bench.

By using the ring as an example we can see how the emery method may be applied to other jewelry articles having curved surfaces.

Chapter 6

Ring Sizing

Making a ring
Reducing ring size
Making a ring larger
Shanking a ring
Sizing stone rings
Ring sizing by flame
Sizing platinum rings

BEGINNING at this point, text references to illustrations are so frequent that the procedures will be outlined in brief. Discussion of various points not essential to the immediate operation will be discussed either before or after the step-by-step instruction.

Making a Ring

Fig. 6.1 illustrates the correct way to use a ring size gauge (Fig. 6.2) to arrive at the exact size when making a ring. Some ring sticks found on the market may not coincide with the method illustrated, there being variations of as much as two sizes. The student is advised to check his size stick with a narrow length of brass, measuring to the size-7 line, shaping and soldering, and then rounding to shape on the heavy steel mandrel. If the gauge on the size stick is accurate, the brass band will measure size 7 on the heavy steel mandrel. A discrepancy in size will show up and thus establish how far off the gauge on the ring size stick really is. This does not mean that the gauge is worthless, but indicates that one or two sizes (whatever the discrepancy amounts to) will have to be allowed for when making rings. For example, a size 7 will measure size 9 on a size stick that is two sizes off, owing to the gauge's being located two sizes too high on the size stick.

And now to proceed:

1. Saw a length of stock measuring from the tip or edge of the ring size stick to the desired size of the ring (size 7, Fig. 6.1).

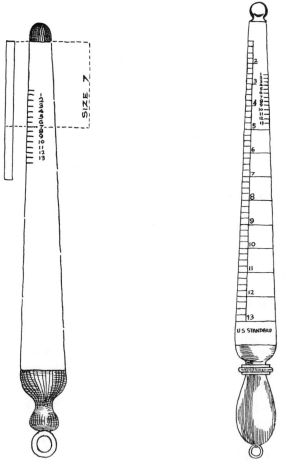

FIG. 6.1. Sizing stock before making a ring.

FIG. 6.2. Ring size gauge, or ring stick.

2. Anneal on the charcoal block by heating the length of metal to a red color and allowing it to cool (Fig. 6.3).

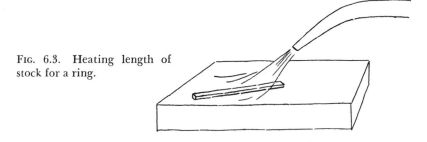

Fig. 6.3. Heating length of stock for a ring.

3. Using bow pliers or a ring shaper, shape the ring, leaving a gap large enough for a file to run through and square the ends (Fig. 6.4).

Fig. 6.4.   Shaping a ring.

4. Square the ends with a barrette file (Fig. 6.5).

5. Bring ends together using half-round pliers (Fig. 6.6). The edges to be joined must be flush.

6. Hold the ring in the electric soldering machine clamp. Set the machine heat gauge at the desired heat and solder (Fig. 6.7). To prepare for soldering, flux the joint (Fig. 6.7A), cut a small square of solder (Fig. 6.7B), apply solder to the joint with the brush (Fig. 6.7C), and solder as shown in Fig. 6.7D. Fig. 6.7E shows the completed joint.

7. After soldering, place the ring in the cold pickle solution for three or four minutes. Then remove the pickle solution by holding the ring under running water.

8. Place the ring on a steel mandrel (Fig. 6.8) and shape by

pounding with a rawhide mallet, reversing the ring on the mandrel from time to time (Fig. 6.9).

9. Remove excess solder on the inside by filing with a #2

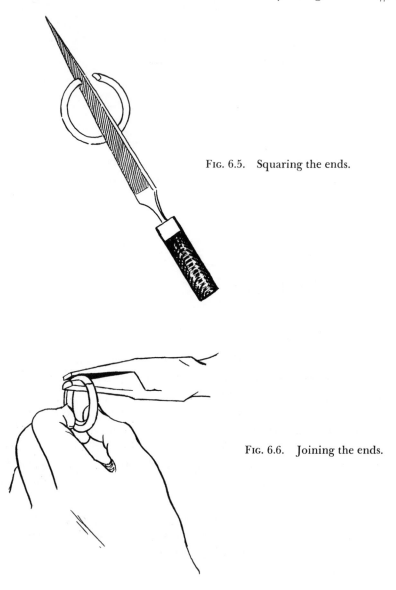

FIG. 6.5.   Squaring the ends.

FIG. 6.6.   Joining the ends.

half-round file. Remove all dents and scratches and finish with a
#4 half-round file (Fig. 6.10).

10. File edges true, using a #2 barrette file and finishing with
a #4 file (Fig. 6.11). Fig. 6.12 shows an alternative method of
filing the sides. This method will not damage the mandrel provided a smooth-sided file is used.

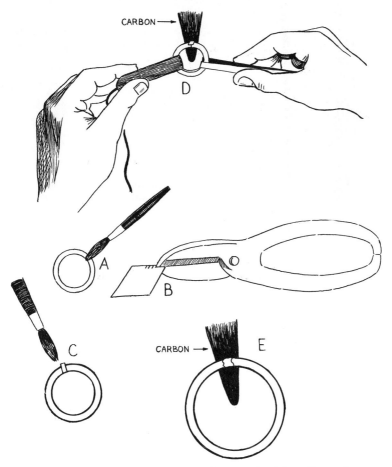

Fɪɢ. 6.7.   Machine-soldering a ring: *A*, fluxing the joint; *B*, cutting square
of solder; *C*, brushing on solder; *D*, soldering; *E*, completed joint.

11. Shape the outside of the ring half round by filing with a #2 barrette file, finishing with a #4 file (Fig. 6.13).

12. Finish sides and outside at the bench with #0 or #00 emery sticks.

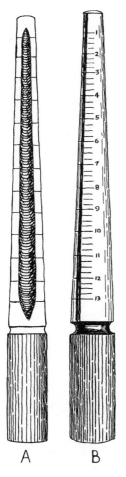

A   B

FIG. 6.8.   Mandrels: *A*, grooved ring mandrel; *B*, smooth or plain mandrel.

13. Buff and polish to a mirror finish. Figs. 6.14, 6.15, 6.16, and 6.17 show methods of buffing. In buffing the inside of the ring, do not try to polish the whole surface at once, or the ring may

be snatched away by the buff. Then the motor will have to be stopped and a new start made. Instead, work with the buffer where it is of smaller diameter than the ring, rotating the ring with the fingers and polishing one section at a time.

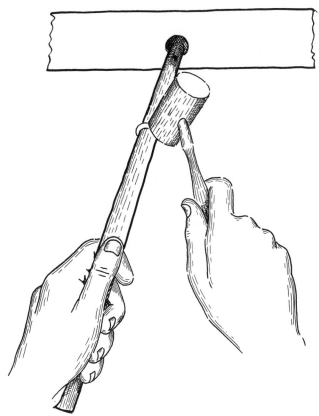

FIG. 6.9.   Shaping the ring on the mandrel.

(*a*) Use tripoli first, with a felt inside ring buff. Wash off the tripoli after buffing.

(*b*) Use rouge next, with a felt inside ring buff.

(*c*) With a very small application of rouge, use a soft clean polishing buff last, for buffing outside surfaces.

14. Boil the ring in the cleaning solution and scrub it with a stiff black brush if necessary.

15. Dip the ring in alcohol and place in sawdust to dry.

Reducing Ring Size

Before any ring is sized, whether larger or smaller, it is well to determine if it has been sized before. To do this, heat the shank slightly, using a flame. As the shank begins to discolor, the previ-

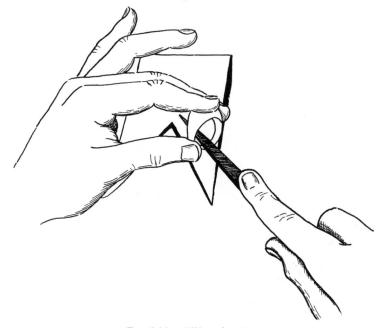

Fig. 6.10.   Filing the ring.

ous joint or joints will show up as thin lines. If the ring is being expanded, saw through at the line. If there are two lines showing, it is often best to remove the old piece and insert an entirely new section. Many minor difficulties may arise if the old piece is used. As one joint is made, the other can shift slightly. If the ring is being made larger it becomes quite a feat to introduce a third piece into the shank and it is certainly not advisable.

To make a ring smaller (in our example, from size 6½ to size 5½) the procedure is as follows:

1. Spread the dividers to measure 1 size, using the gauge on the side of the ring size stick.

2. Heat the ring at the center of the shank to locate a previous joint, if any.

3. With the dividers, mark off the size on the center of the ring shank, beginning with or including any previous joint.

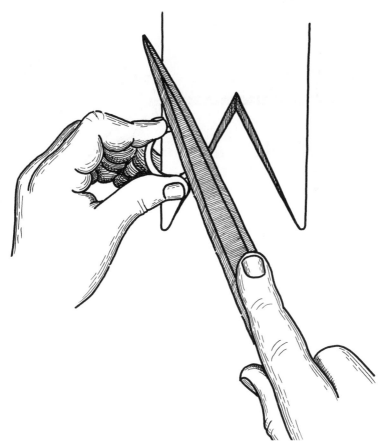

Fig. 6.11.   Filing the soldered joint of the ring.

4. Saw out the size. Saw to the outside of the marked line to make sure that the maximum size is taken out. In sizing rings, keep in mind that the ring must be kept on the small side. After soldering, if the ring measures 5⅜, it will expand slightly in pounding and filing. This is a better condition than to have the ring come out at size 5⅝.

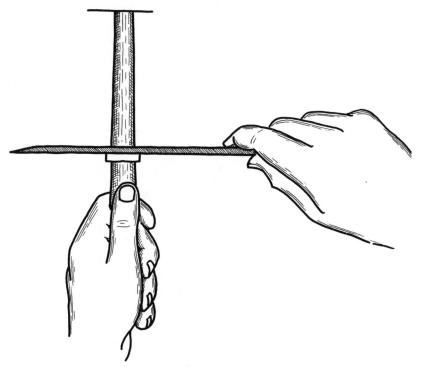

FIG. 6.12.   Filing the sides of the ring.

5. Square the ends with a barrette file.

6. Bring the ends together with half-round pliers, forming a closely fitted joint.

7. Flux the joint.

8. Cut a small square of solder (matching the karat) and apply to the carbon.

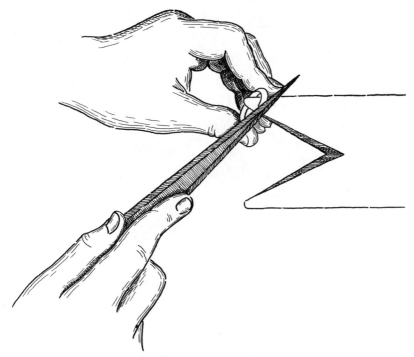

FIG. 6.13.   Shaping the outside of the ring.

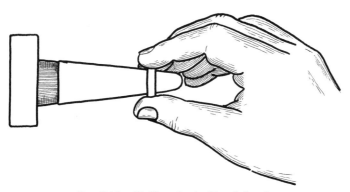

FIG. 6.14.   Buffing the inside of the ring.

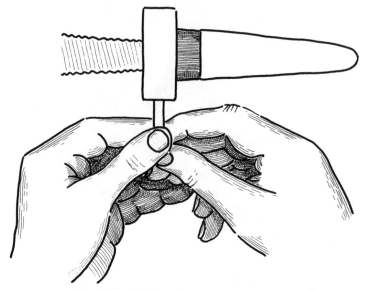

FIG. 6.15.   Buffing the outside of the ring.

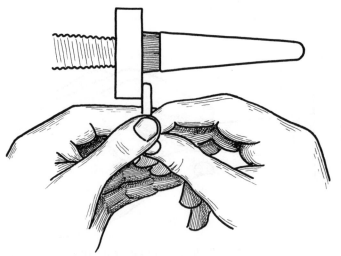

FIG. 6.16.   Buffing the sides of the ring on the side of a solid felt wheel.

9. Hold the ring by the machine clamp and solder, using heat according to the thickness of the shank.

10. After soldering, place the ring in the pickle solution to remove flux and oxidation. Leave the ring in the cold pickle solution for three or four minutes, then remove. Wash the pickle solution off under running water.

11. Place the ring on the mandrel and shape by pounding with the rawhide mallet.

FIG. 6.17.   Buffing the ring.

12. Remove the excess solder on inside of ring by filing. Shape again by pounding.

13. File the sides flat over the joint to match the complete shank.

14. Shape the outside of the shank by filing over the joint.

15. Finish the sides and outside with an emery stick, grit #0 or #00.

16. Buff and polish to a mirror finish.

17. Clean rouge from the ring by boiling it in the cleaning solution.

18. Remove the ring and dip it in alcohol. Dry it in sawdust.

Making a Ring Larger

In enlarging a ring, e.g., from size 8 to size 9½, the following steps would be carried out.

1. Spread dividers to measure 1½ sizes (scant).
2. Mark off this length on the sizing stock and saw out the piece.
3. Square the ends with a barrette file (Fig. 6.18).
4. Heat the ring shank to locate previous joints, if any.
5. Saw the shank (at the previous joint, if any).

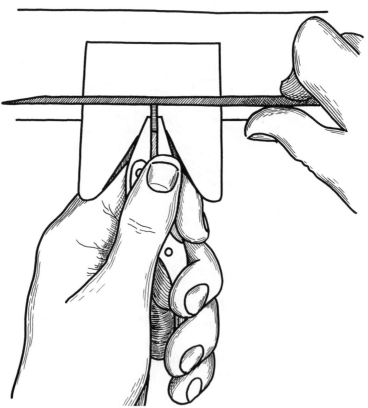

Fig. 6.18.   Using the barrette file.

6. Open the shank by bending outward with half-round pliers.

7. Square the ends to match the section to be inserted.

8. Solder the joint in the manner shown in Fig. 6.19.

9. Shape the shank to fit snugly at the other joint.

10. Solder the second joint, leaving the thick part of the piece on the outside. This will eliminate much inside filing.

11. Place the ring in the pickle solution; wash and dry.

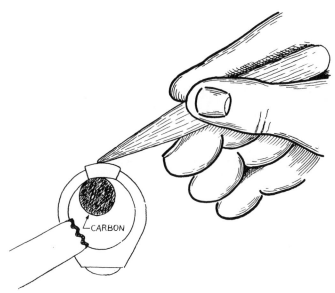

Fig. 6.19.   Soldering the new joint.

12. Shape the ring on the mandrel by pounding, reversing it from time to time to prevent the ring from measuring larger on one side than the other.

13. File to shape.

14. Buff and polish.

15. Clean and dry as previously explained.

Note (a): In checking the size the bottom of the shank should touch the line marked $9\frac{1}{2}$. Reverse the ring and check the other side. This should measure the same.

Note (*b*): An alternative way to fit a joint is shown in Fig. 6.20A, B, and C. This method provides a firmer joint and a more secure one. First saw out the joint as shown at *A*. At *B* note that the joint to be inserted is tapered at both ends. The ring surfaces are shaped with a small square file to receive the joint. *C* shows the joint in place and ready to be soldered.

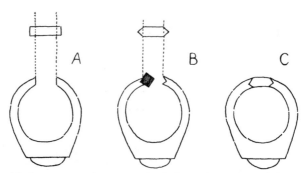

F ɪ ɢ. 6.20.   Fitting a new piece in a ring: *A*, sawing out the joint; *B*, taper of the ring and the joint; *C*, joint in place.

Shanking a Ring

1. Saw out the worn section of the shank (Fig. 6.21A and B).
2. Straighten the section with pliers (Fig. 6.21C, 1).
3. Place the section on the stock and mark off the length (Fig. 6.21C, 2). The length of the stock piece should be slightly smaller than the section removed from the ring, because the ring will expand as it is shaped, filed, and buffed. Saw out the piece and square the ends.
4. Solder in the manner explained above under Making a Ring Larger. Fig. 6.21D shows how the piece may be held. Fig. 6.22 shows how to shape the inserted shank with bow pliers, preparatory to soldering the opposite side.
5. Shape the ring on the mandrel.
6. File.
7. Polish.
8. Wash and dry.

Sizing Stone Rings

Procedures are the same in sizing stone rings, but with added precautions taken to protect the stone. All stones except diamonds, rubies, and sapphires should be considered extremely perishable

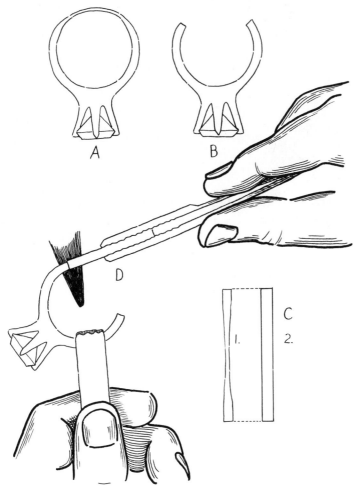

Fig. 6.21. Replacing worn section of a ring shank: *A*, worn ring; *B*, ring with section cut out; *C*, matching length; *D*, soldering.

and may be wrapped with wet cotton (Figs. 6.23 and 6.24) or submerged in wet sand for flame-soldering (Fig. 6.25A, B, C, D).
Machine work is quicker and the danger of heat damaging the

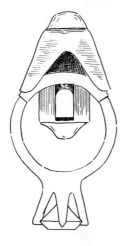

FIG. 6.22.   Shaping the shank insert.

stone is greatly reduced. On most thin-shanked ladies' rings, wrapping is not necessary. On heavier, wide shanks, wrapping is necessary because of the greater heat required to flow the solder.
When a stone is wrapped, even greater heat is demanded. On any
doubtful job, always wrap the stone.

Care must be taken not to crack or loosen the stone in bending
and shaping. Every stone ring must be checked after completing

FIG. 6.23.   Stone wrapped in wet
cotton.

FIG. 6.24.   Enlarging a ring with the
stone wrapped.

the job. Opening or closing shanks sometimes creates pressures that may crack the stone even after the job is completed. Discretion should be used, especially when the job requires great expansion or reduction in size. It often happens that the stone will not stand the alteration. This can be decided beforehand, thus avoiding trouble.

Ring Sizing by Flame

1. Procedures are the same as in machine-soldering. Prepare the edges to be joined for soldering.

2. Hold the ring in soldering tweezers.

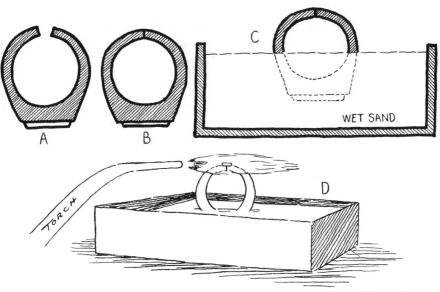

Fig. 6.25.   Submerging a stone in wet sand: *A, B, C, D,* stages of soldering.

3. Adjust the flame so that only blue is seen. It is not necessary or desirable to concentrate the flame to a fine point, as this creates a danger of melting. A slow steady heat is wanted, so a broader blue flame is just right (Fig. 6.25D). The flame may be applied to the joint gradually at first by waving back and forth. As the

flux and solder become set and the heat is building up, leave the flame directly over the join until the solder flows through. The advantage of flame-soldering is in better control of the solder. The solder can be seen and directed to flow where desired, since it will always follow the most concentrated point of heat.

Figures 6.25A, B, C, and D show the successive steps in preparing a stone ring for flame-soldering. The substance shown in the container (Fig. 6.25D) is pure white sand that is saturated with water. The stone is submerged as shown in the cross section (Fig. 6.25C). The wet sand serves the double purpose of protecting the stone from damage and of holding the ring in a steady position during the soldering operation.

During a day, when there are many such ring-sizing jobs to be done, several rings can be prepared for soldering and placed in position in the sand container. Soldering all of the rings, one after another, will save valuable time.

Sizing Platinum Rings

Platinum solder may be bought in varying degrees of melting points. The higher the designation, the more heat is indicated in the soldering operation. The selection of the proper solder may be governed by the marking inside the shank of the platinum ring.

The procedure of soldering is the same as that of any other soldering operation except for the fact that a much higher degree of heat is used. In fact, the degree of heat is so high that the metal will become impossible to look at with the naked eye. Dark glasses are used not only to protect the eye but to determine what is going on when the solder flows. Great care must be used to remove the heat the instant solder flows for there is constant danger of melting the shank. If one is adept in ordinary gold soldering, there is no reason not to attempt the solder of platinum.

This warning must be observed: **Never solder platinum without using a good pair of dark glasses.** This means dark glasses, not merely tinted lenses. Be sure nothing is behind the flame that is even slightly inflammable, for the heat required carries much farther than heat used in normal soldering. It is suggested that practice with an old platinum ring (discarded or otherwise of no value except for its platinum content) be repeated until the operation is mastered.

After successfully completing this phase, the shank may be rounded and filed or trimmed in the usual manner but with this one emphasis: rely more on emery sticks, particularly the fine ones, than the final polishing done on the buff. The special platinum rouge used on the buff will remove the solder quickly making the joint more distinguishable than it should be. Therefore do not over-buff at the polishing motor, but polish more with the emery stick so that a minimum of buffing with the motor is required.

This soldered line after buffing on the motor is such a worrisome factor that many jewelry repairmen never use solder except as a last resort. They have found that the flawless way to size platinum rings is to weld them using a bit of the platinum from the shank (if made smaller) or using the nearest match to the quality of platinum in the shank.

The operation is accomplished in this manner. Using side cutting pliers a sliver of platinum may be trimmed from an end section of platinum shank (usually from the piece removed). By placing this bit of platinum on a bench vise and hammering as seen in Fig. 6.26A, the metal will be reduced to a paper-thin sheet of platinum that may be inserted in the closed ring shank. See Fig. 6.26B.

The joint may be fluxed prior to applying an intense pencil flame. Being very thin, the piece of platinum will tend to melt before the melting point of the shank is reached. The edges may be seen to curl, then gradually melt and blend with the shank as shown in Figs. 6.26C, 6.26D, and 6.26E. The joint is welded and when pounded on the mandrel will be found to be as strong as any part of the shank, a factor that proves it to be superior to the soldering method. File and polish, and note that there is no solder joint to attract the attention of anyone.

One caution more: the melting points of the paper-thin piece and the mother-shank become very close at the final instant of spreading (see Fig. 6.26E). It will take practice to develop this skill without melting the shank.

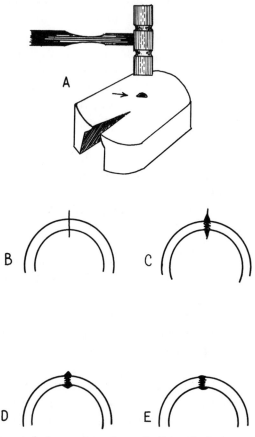

FIG. 6.26.   Sizing a platinum ring: *A*, small piece of platinum; *B*, paper-thin hammered platinum; *C*, beginning to melt; *D*, melting; *E*, the welded joint.

Chapter 7

Joint, Catch, and Pinstem Work

Repairing bar pins—hard solder
Repairing bar pins—soft solder

To GAIN experience in the repair of bar pins, brooches, and all miscellaneous pins requiring joint, catch, and pinstem replacement or repair, a simple bar pin can be made from brass stock.

Repairing Bar Pins—Hard Solder

1. Saw from raw stock a bar ⅜ × 1½ inches (Fig. 7.1A).
2. File all edges square.

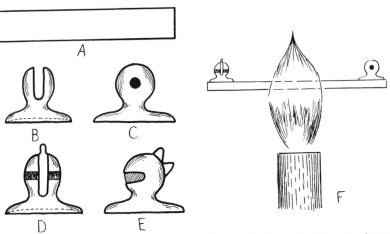

FIG. 7.1. Making a bar pin: *A*, bar; *B, C,* joint; *D, E,* catch; *F,* heating bar to flow solder.

107

3. Bevel the edges of the top side slightly.

4. Line-finish both sides with a coarse-grit emery to remove all dents and scratches. Finish with #0 or #00 emery, leaving a smooth line-finish running lengthwise. To line-finish, rub the bar back and forth over flat emery paper or an emery stick, taking care to keep the same direction so that lines will appear perfectly par-

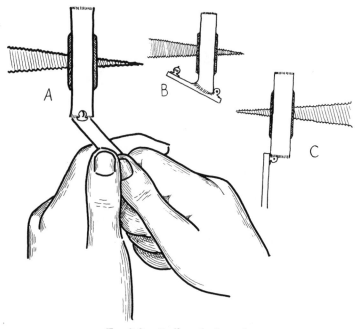

FIG. 7.2.   Buffing the bar pin.

allel with the edges of the bar. The last strokes should be forward to insure uniformity of lines.

5. On the back of the bar, locate the positions for the *joint* and the *catch*. The joint is placed to the right, the catch to the left (Fig. 7.1F).

6. With a file, scratch the surface to be soldered. Solder flows better on a clean, rough surface.

7. With a file, scratch and generally roughen the surface of the

cup under the joint and of that under the catch (Fig. 7.1B, C, D, E).

8. Place the bar on an asbestos pad or charcoal block.

9. Apply flux and a small square of solder to the prepared spots on the bar; flux the bottom of the joint and that of the catch.

10. With a blowpipe or oxygen-gas torch apply a broad blue flame to the bar and allow the solder to flow.

11. With tweezers place the joint and the catch each in its proper position.

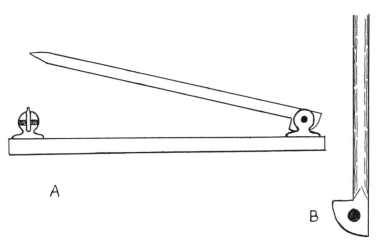

Fig. 7.3. Fitting the pinstem.

12. Apply the flame again until the solder flows all around the base of the joint and that of the catch. (*Caution:* Too much heat will melt the joint and the catch, since they are much smaller than the bar.) Heat the center of the bar first, gradually moving the flame to the joint, then to the catch. When solder flows, remove the flame instantly.

13. While hot, plunge the pin into the pickle solution. (Pickle solution works better and faster while the article is hot.)

14. Wash the pin and dry it; buff the back to remove all re-

maining stains and to restore the appearance of the joint and the catch (Fig. 7.2A, B, and C).

15. Select a pinstem of proper length. The point should engage well into the catch and extend slightly on the other side (about $\frac{1}{16}$ inch). It should not extend beyond the edge of the bar pin (Fig. 7.3A).

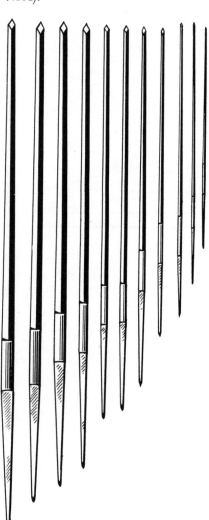

FIG. 7.4.　Broaches.

16. Check the hole size of the pinstem and of the joint for comparative size (Fig. 7.3B).

17. Use a broach (Fig. 7.4) to broach out the smaller hole or holes to size (Fig. 7.5).

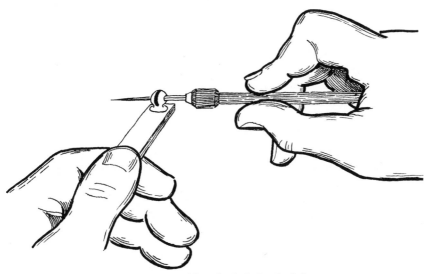

Fig. 7.5.   Broaching the hole in the joint.

18. Select wire slightly larger than the holes—sterling, nickel, brass, or gold as the pin demands.

19. Roll-file to a gradual taper (Fig. 7.6) fitting the wire in the

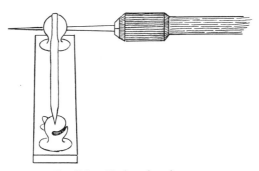

Fig. 7.6.   Fitting the pinstem.

hole from right to left. The wire must fit tightly in the joint and be barely free in the pinstem hole. It may be necessary at this point to broach out the hole in the pinstem and make it slightly larger.

20. Place the joint and pinstem in position; run in the wire

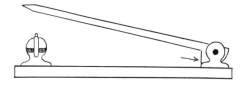

FIG. 7.7.   Testing the fit of a pinstem.

and test the pinstem for freedom, noting at this point if the pinstem will engage in the catch (Fig. 7.7).

21. If the pinstem will not engage, remove and file away metal as shown in Fig. 7.8.

22. Allow a slight degree of tension, so that the stem will not engage in the catch unless it is pressed downward slightly (Fig. 7.9).

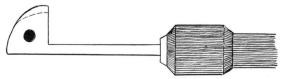

FIG. 7.8.   Where to file the pinstem.

23. Snip the wire ends close to the joint, leaving just enough metal to form rivets. Use side cutters to snip the wire.

24. Place the bar pin on the bench block (Figs. 7.10 and 7.11) and rivet by using several light taps with a light steel riveting hammer. Use the riveting end (wedge-shaped) until the rivet has safely spread over the hole; then use the flat end of the hammer to finish

FIG. 7.9.   Tension in the pinstem.

the rivet. Do this with several light taps, striking the rivet from different angles. This is done by slightly changing position of the hammer and rotating the strokes in a circular manner. The result will be a smooth, polished rivet which need not be filed.

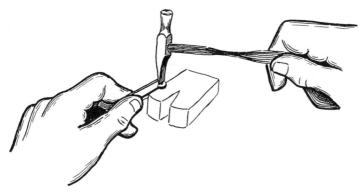

FIG. 7.10.   Riveting the pin.

25. To add tension to the pinstem, place snipe-nose pliers just in front of the joint and bend upward slightly. This will ensure that the pinstem will remain in the slot of the catch even though the safety mechanism is not closed (Fig. 7.12).

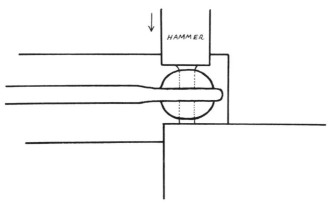

FIG. 7.11.   Heading the rivet of the pin.

26. The front of the pin may receive its final finish by buffing to a high polish or it may be smoothly line-finished.

Before doing any hard-solder work on a bar pin or brooch, it is advisable to examine closely the nature of the article. If it is a solid piece of metal there is little danger of spoiling it. If, however, the article is a thin shell or if it is composed of fine filigree work, then extreme caution must be used to avoid overheating or

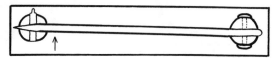

FIG. 7.12.   The riveted pin.

melting the metal. Enamel surfaces must be observed, for frequently the melting point of the enamel is very close to the melting point of the solder, and it can very easily flow out of its groove. Many enameled pieces can be safely soldered by careful handling of the flame. In some instances the enamel may be so close to the solder joint that the electric soldering machine is the safest method, thanks to the speed of soldering by electric arc.

Repairing Bar Pins—Soft Solder

1. Saw, file, and line-finish the bar, as explained above under Repairing Bar Pins—Hard Solder.

2. Prepare the area for soldering as explained under Repairing Bar Pins—Hard Solder.

3. Apply soft-solder flux to the areas and place a small amount of soft solder at an inverted joint.

4. Hold the joint in soldering tweezers and wave it back and forth over an alcohol flame until the solder flows and fills the cup-shaped base. Repeat the procedure on the catch.

5. Place the joint and the catch each in its position while holding the bar with tweezers. Pass the entire assembly over the alcohol flame, and flow solder at both joints (Fig. 7.1F).

6. Clean as explained above under Repairing Bar Pins—Hard

Solder. It is not necessary to place soft-soldered work in the pickle solution. Polish, wash, and dry the pin.

One good rule to follow in soft-soldering joints and catches is to use the original method of soldering. If the piece of jewelry was originally soft-soldered, there is obviously no decision to be made. But, if the original was hard-soldered, then by no means should one consider using soft solder, which would be a half measure at best. If the manufacturer saw fit to hard-solder the joints, the repairman should do likewise. Soft-soldering joints and catches on a valuable piece of jewelry should be done only if hard-soldering is impossible, and then only with the customer's knowledge and sanction.

To determine how an original joint was soldered, use a graver to make a cut in the broken area. Soft solder is very soft, and being either bismuth or lead, will show a white color; whereas hard solder will offer more resistance to the graver.

If an article for repair has been soft-soldered when it should have been hard-soldered, then it behooves the repairman to remove the soft solder. (For the method of doing this, see Chapter 16, Solutions and Formulae.) Then proceed to do the job correctly, using hard solder.

Chapter 8

Chain and Link Repair

Handling jump rings, spring rings, links
Chain soldering
Chain soldering with the electric machine
Chain soldering by flame
Repairing worn links or rings

THE MANIPULATION of jump rings, spring rings, and links can be a source of annoyance unless they are handled with the proper tools. By using incorrect pliers the rings can be marred or lost as they slip out of the jaws of pliers. It would be well to study this relatively simple operation and begin with correct habits (if just learning); if already experienced in the trade, perhaps present methods may be improved by switching to parallel snipe-nose pliers with smooth jaws.

Handling Jump Rings, Spring Rings, and Links

First, see Fig. 8.1. The parallel pliers have a firm grip on the jump ring as the opening operation begins. In Fig. 8.2, the opening is taking place and the grip on the ring is just as firm and

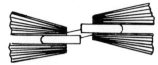

FIG. 8.1. Gripping the jump ring.   FIG. 8.2. Opening the jump ring.

116

steady as it was in Fig. 8.1. In Fig. 8.3, the opening is completed. Note the position of the ends of the jump rings are still parallel —or, if they are not parallel in actual practice every time, that section of the ring does not bend because it is being held firm by the pliers. When the ends are brought back together they are flush.

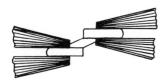

FIG. 8.3.   The opening is completed.   FIG. 8.4.   A poor grip, using conventional snipe-nose pliers.

In Fig. 8.4, we see the same bending operation using conventional snipe-nose pliers. Obviously we do not have to illustrate the same bending operations as we did using parallel pliers in Figs. 8.2 and 8.3. The enlarged view clearly shows that the situation invites slipping, twisting, and turning with a loss of time as an inevitable result.

FIG. 8.5.   Jump ring marred by conventional pliers.

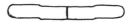

Fig. 8.5 shows how jump rings or any link can look at the end of the operation using conventional snipe-nose pliers. In Fig. 8.6 is shown the opening and closing grip on the small connecting ring of a conventional spring ring, using parallel pliers.

FIG. 8.6.   Opening connecting ring to spring ring.

For exceptionally small jump rings or links it is worthwhile to alter the size of the tips of the parallel pliers, if they seem to be bulky or large in handling. The pliers may be softened by heating the tips, then as the jaws are held firmly together, reduced in size by filing or grinding using an emery wheel. Using emery sticks, the tips may be polished and re-hardened.

Chain Soldering

For practice in chain soldering, one may start by using simple jump rings (sterling). These are inexpensive and can be used again. Starting with the largest size, solder the joints, using the smallest possible amount of solder—just enough to hold securely. The reason for using a minimum of solder is an obvious one when the situation is studied. An excess of solder will demand filing and polishing. No excess means no filing and no polishing, except a slight touch to restore brilliance.

Oval jump rings more nearly resemble chain links. Starting with the largest available size, solder the first joint. Then join the second jump ring to the first; join the third to the second, and so on, until a chain of eight to ten links is made. Examine the joints to see if a correct amount of solder is being used. Just as in sizing rings, it is important to carefully see that all joints are flush to insure strong smooth joints.

After some skill has been acquired soldering the largest rings, gradually reduce the size of the rings until the smallest available jump ring is soldered with ease.

So far only a degree of soldering skill has been gained; the real problem is soldering an actual chain with all its peculiarities. There is nothing consistent about chain soldering for chains may be of any shape or size. Even the largest, apparently simple jobs may be hard to handle because of an unusual twist or bend given to the shape of each link in the manufacture. Naturally the successful job is one in which the contour of the link is not destroyed, but matches all the others perfectly. Also, the soldered joint should be so carefully hidden (or camouflaged) that it is not detectable.

If the beginner has chains of many sizes with which to practice, it would be wise to gradually reduce the size of the chains he works on, following the same technique.

One rather surprising reaction to watch for is this: when the tiniest chains are placed in position for soldering and the usual hot bed is brought closer and closer to the joint, the solder often flows without the flame ever touching the metal. This is because the amount of solder required is hardly larger than a pinpoint. The heat generated in a hot bed is of much greater intensity than any other kind, inasmuch as very little of it is dissipated or lost; rather, it is concentrated in such a way that it seems to build up and become increasingly intense. Great care and watchfulness are demanded at this point, for melting a section of small chain is quite an easy thing to do.

Many chains brought in for soldering are too inexpensive to bother with or may be worn out. The worn-out chain in particular can be a source of extreme annoyance, a loss of time and money. Small worn-out chains may be hard to detect, since the worn or thin links are not readily visible. Close examination with the average loupe, however, will show the true condition.

Often a worn-out chain is repaired very easily, only to be returned ten minutes afterward because it has come apart again. Of course it has come apart at a different link, but the customer is usually under the impression that the original break (which is now the strongest link in the chain) has parted again. The repairman would be doing the customer and himself a favor by suggesting the purchase of a new chain rather than attempting to repair such an article. After all, a repairman is judged by the quality of his work. Why jeopardize a good reputation?

Chain Soldering with the Electric Machine

1. Connect the broken chain, using the broken link as shown in Fig. 8.7.

2. Bring broken ends together, using two pairs of snipe-nose pliers.

3. Hold the broken link separate from the others, using the machine clamp.

4. Flux the joint.

5. Apply a small corner of solder, just enough to flow through, leaving no excess.

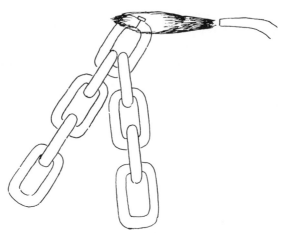

FIG. 8.7.   Soldering a broken link.

6. Set the heat gauge to a low heat and solder (Fig. 8.8).
7. Place in the pickle solution.
8. Wash and dry.
9. Restore the finish.

FIG. 8.8.   Machine-soldering a link.

It is sometimes possible to solder and restore the appearance of small chains without using the polishing machine. After soldering, place the chain in the pickle solution to remove oxidization. Then lay the chain on a flat surface and scrub the soldered area briskly, using a moistened stiff-bristle hand brush with baking soda. If the joint is not badly discolored, this will restore the appearance. If, however, the area still looks dull and more attention is indicated, the buffing operation (at the polishing motor) cannot be avoided. Carefully wrap the section needing attention around any smooth piece of wood—the base of an emery hand buff will serve very well. Holding the excess chain in one hand (firmly, so that no slack is evident on the section to be presented to the bristle wheel brush) lightly touch the chain to a rouged buff (tripoli is rarely needed). Do not overpolish, because it is possible to complete the job only to find that the section you have polished is more brilliant than the rest of the chain.

For soldering extremely fine chains by machine, the square-cornered carbon may be used (Fig. 9.4). Place paper over the carbon, allowing only the portion that is to be soldered to touch. With the copper point, touch the joint and solder instantly, using a very low heat.

Chain Soldering by Flame

1. Prepare the chain in the same manner as for machine soldering.

2. Lay the chain on the asbestos pad or charcoal block.

3. Have the link to be soldered pulled away from the others (Fig. 8.7).

4. Apply the flux and a small corner of solder.

5. With the blowpipe or oxygen-gas torch, direct a small blue flame about $\frac{1}{2}$ inch from the joint.

6. Move the hot bed gradually to the joint, to flow the solder. In some instances, on small chains, solder may flow before the flame actually touches the joint. This method results in less oxidation and can be refinished with ease.

7. Put in the pickle solution, clean, and refinish as directed for machine-soldering.

So far, we have discussed only simple link chains of various sizes. These will account for the great majority of chain-soldering jobs, although there are many different styles and types of chains. Even link chains vary considerably in shape and design, though the method of repair will be the same for all.

The really fancy varieties of chains, such as snake, rope, and the rest, will present some very tricky situations that require great dexterity with the soldering torch or machine. For instance, a snake chain should be soldered with minimum heat to prevent a frozen or stiff section around the joint. A minimum of solder and a minimum of flux are used here, for too much solder causes the joint to freeze and too much flux causes the solder to flow exces-

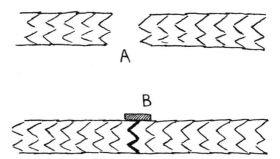

Fig. 8.9.   Snake chain: *A*, broken link; *B*, ready to solder.

sively, again causing the joint section to freeze. It might appear that to solder a snake chain successfully is little short of a miracle, but such is not the case. Careful application of flux and a minimum amount of solder are the most important points to observe.

To solder a snake chain, a soldering block may be used to great advantage, since the chain may be pinned (with short, bent sections of steel binding wire) to the pad. The carbon pencil is handy for this job if the machine is used. The flame is a very good medium for this job, since once the chain is pinned in position, there is nothing to disturb it or cause the correct position to shift.

Fig. 8.9A shows a broken snake chain. Fig. 8.9B shows the chain fitted together and ready to solder on the asbestos pad.

Broken rope chains may be fitted into position, pinned to the pad, and soldered in much the same manner. Designs will vary of course, and one will be required to think out the situation in advance before haphazardly beginning to solder.

One job frequently encountered is the snake watch bracelet which has broken at one of the tips or where the ends are soldered to the fittings. To simply solder the two ends is often quite useless since this particular spot seems to get more action or stress than any other section of the bracelet. It will often break again shortly after soldering. The most satisfactory way to do this job is to heat the fitting that still contains the very short end or section of the snake chain. As the melting point of the solder is reached, force out the useless end and discard it. Place the good end in the fitting and solder as it was originally done when the bracelet was manufactured. Now the bracelet is like new, with no solder joint, although it is slightly shorter. Often the difference in length is not noticeable, and if it is, the adjustable catch usually takes care of the situation. It is a good idea to tell the customer just what the problem is before soldering. When she finds that her bracelet can be repaired without making a visible solder joint, though it becomes slightly shorter, she is usually well pleased.

Repairing Worn Links or Rings

1. With a small file, roughen the area to be filled (Fig. 8.10A).
2. Apply flux to the area.
3. Apply enough solder to fill the worn gap (Fig. 8.10B).
4. With the flame gradually build up the heat until the solder flows and fills in the gap (Fig. 8.10C).
5. Place in the pickle solution.
6. Buff and clean.

Note: The machine can also be used for this work, although solder can be better directed by using the flame.

Fig. 8.11A, B, C shows another method of repairing a worn link. The worn section is cut out; the two ends are brought together and soldered.

Fig. 8.12 shows how to repair a link or small ring with a considerable amount of metal worn away as shown at *A*. The section is removed (*B*) and a new section soldered in place (*C*).

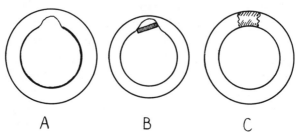

FIG. 8.10.   Repairing a worn link, I: *A*, link; *B*, filling worn area; *C*, gap filled with solder.

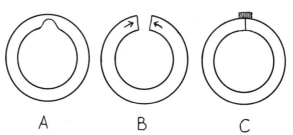

FIG. 8.11.   Repairing a worn link, II: *A*, link; *B*, section cut out; *C*, soldering ends.

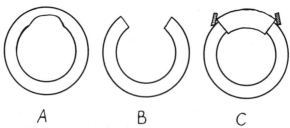

FIG. 8.12.   Repairing a worn link, III: *A*, link; *B*, section removed; *C*, soldering in new section.

Chapter 9

Spectacle-Frame Repair

Repairing bridges
Repairing nosepieces
Repairing temples

IN SOME STATES the repair of spectacle frames by jewelry repairmen is illegal. It is required that the repair of frames be supervised or made by an optometrist or optician. For years customers have associated the optometrist profession with jewelry stores, and many optometrists' offices are located in or next to jewelry stores. As a result there is a steady flow of customers who bring their eyeglasses to jewelry stores to be repaired or for part replacement.

The actual repair of spectacle frames is not a difficult task for one well trained in soldering. The care of the lenses and the correct adjustment of the frames after soldering are points that should be carefully observed.

Repair procedures for bridges, nosepieces, and temples are given below.

Repairing Bridges

1. To solder broken bridges, first remove the lenses by using a screwdriver (Fig. 9.1) to loosen the side screws (Fig. 9.2). Before

FIG. 9.1. Screwdriver.
125

removing lenses, rub Chinese white on each lens at the screw position. With a pegwood point or rubber marker, draw a line at
this joint so that, when lenses are replaced, the same position will
be found (Fig. 9.2).

2. Clean and flux the broken ends.

FIG. 9.2.   Removing a lens.

3. Lay solder on top of the carbon; hold the frame as shown in
Fig. 9.3 or Fig. 9.4. Solder·the joint.

4. Place the frame in the pickle solution.

5. Buff with a bristle brush lightly rouged.

6. Wash in cleaning solution.

7. Dip in alcohol and allow to dry.

8. Replace lenses, temples, and screws.

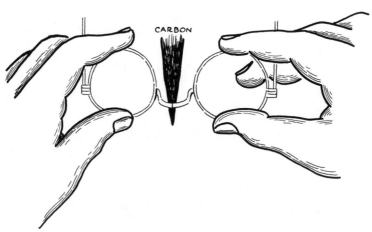

FIG. 9.3.   Machine-soldering a bridge.

9. Check frames to make sure lenses are in line and frames are straight.

Repairing Nosepieces

1. Wrap the celluloid pads with wet cotton.

2. Clamp the frames to the asbestos pad, using short pieces of steel binding wire (Fig. 9.5).

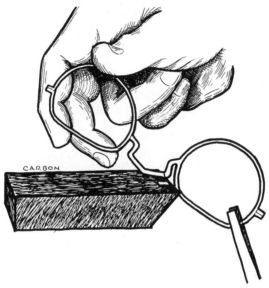

Fig. 9.4.   Holding the bridge in position.

3. With optical pliers, bend outward the extreme curve in the nosepiece just enough to give better clearance and easier handling.

4. Prepare contact points for soldering.

5. Holding nosepieces in soldering tweezers, apply a thin blue flame to the joint until the solder flows. Great care must be taken not to overheat. There is danger of loosening the bridge if it happens to be close to the contact area, as is often the case.

6. Remove from the asbestos pad and place in the pickle solution.

7. Buff the soldered area with a stiff bristle brush slightly

rouged. Do not overbuff: there is danger of wearing through the plating.

8. Wash in cleaning solution.

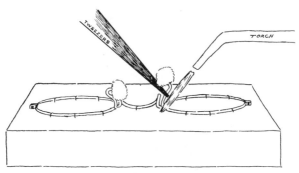

FIG. 9.5.   Soldering a nosepiece.

9. Dip in alcohol; place in sawdust to dry.

10. Replace lenses, temples, and screws. Wipe lenses with lens cleaning tissue or cloth.

Note: The same procedure is followed when using the machine. The frames are held in the clamp, and the nosepiece is held with soldering tweezers. Machine soldering requires two steady hands, flame soldering only one.

Repairing Temples

1. Remove the broken temple from the frame.
2. Clean the broken ends.

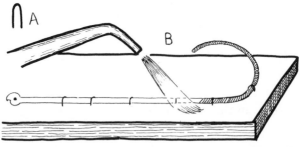

FIG. 9.6.   Soldering a temple: *A*, wire clamp; *B*, applying flame.

3. Clamp with binding wire to the asbestos pad, fitting the two pieces close and straight (Fig. 9.6).

4. Flux the joint and lay a small square of solder directly over the break.

5. With a small blue flame, solder.

6. Place the temple in the pickle solution.

7. Buff lightly, using a little rouge.

8. Clean and allow to dry in sawdust.

9. Replace the temple, and screw. Reshape the nosepiece to match the other side.

Note: Allow solder to make a slight bulge over the joint for added strength. If the solder joint is dressed down flush with the temple surface, it will be the weakest spot and will be apt to break at the slightest strain.

Chapter 10

Hinge Work

THE JEWELRY repairman is frequently called upon to perform major or minor repairs upon articles of hinge construction. Many old pieces of jewelry have numerous hinged arrangements that become badly worn, needing complete or partial replacement.

To illustrate the repair of hinged pieces of jewelry a simple locket will be used, since the principle of all hinge work is essentially the same. Also, for practice work the locket may be the easiest article to obtain.

Before beginning this work it is necessary to have a wide selection of hollow wire on hand, since hinge work demands quite a range of sizes.

Follow closely the step-by-step procedures and there will be little difficulty in repairing such articles.

1. Remove the contents of the locket—pictures, ornaments, or any filling.

2. Select hollow wire with a diameter matching the old or worn parts. The hinge consists of three joints or sections of hollow wire and the hinge pin (Fig. 10.1A-F). The two outer sections of wire are soldered to one side of the locket; the single or center section is soldered to the other side of the locket.

3. Mark off on the new wire the lengths of the old sections.

4. Make slight marks or scratches on the locket showing the correct positions for the new pieces.

5. Remove the hinge pin, using a pin pusher.

6. Dip the article in the antioxidizing solution and ignite. (See Chapter 16, Solutions and Formulae.)

7. Remove the old wire by melting the solder and lifting off
the sections with tweezers. Use the flame, laying the article on the
asbestos pad.

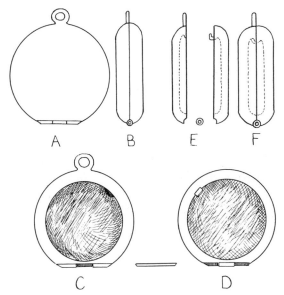

FIG. 10.1.   Hinged locket.

8. Saw out the new sections.

9. Prepare the grooves to receive the new joints. This means
filing the grooves clean and flowing fresh solder in them. To do
this filing, a joint file (Fig. 10.2A, B) is used as shown in Fig. 10.3.

10. Lay the two sections in position and solder one side of the
locket (Fig. 10.4A).

11. Lay the one section in position and solder the other side
(Fig. 10.4B).

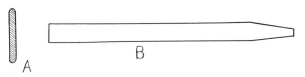

FIG. 10.2.   A joint file.

12. Try the center section between the two outer sections for fit. Slight filing alterations may be made to improve the fit.

13. Close the locket and check the fit and alignment of all sections.

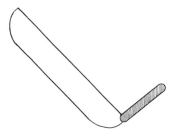

Fɪɢ. 10.3.   Using the joint file.

14. If one section appears out of position, it will be necessary to reheat the area and nudge the section as the solder flows. Try the fit again.

15. When satisfactory, select a pin to fit, or roll-file a pin (Fig. 10.5A). It becomes necessary to broach out the holes in the joints to give them a slight taper to receive the pin (Fig. 10.5B).

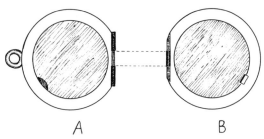

A   B

Fɪɢ. 10.4.   Sections of the locket.

16. Place the pin in position and close the locket to test the closing action before cutting off (Fig. 10.5C).

17. If satisfactory, cut the pin close to the locket (Fig. 10.5D).

18. File away excessive metal to conform with the contour of the locket (Fig. 10.5E).

19. Buff, clean, and dry the completed job (Fig. 10.5F).

Many jobs arise where the hole in the center section has become oversized through wear. It is necessary to replace only this section, using the same pin, provided the pin is not worn thin. Often an

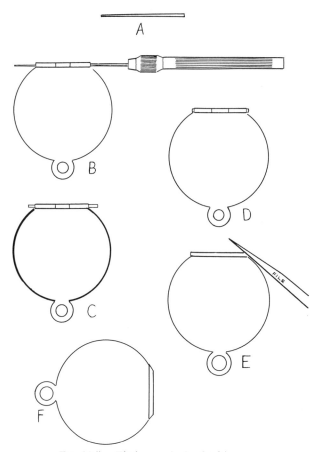

Fig. 10.5.   Fitting a pin in the hinge.

oversized hole in the center section will cause a faulty closing action when the lids are pressed together. A new section corrects this unless the lip is worn where the two lids snap together.

To correct a worn lip, the edge may be made sharper by cutting the groove a little deeper with a graver. If the lip is worn away entirely, a piece of stock should be soldered over the area and trimmed to the required shape.

The tongue that snaps over the lip may not engage properly, making it impossible to close the lids. In some instances it is possible to bend the tongue so that it does engage securely. It could be that the tongue is too badly worn and another must be soldered to it.

Caution: Bad engagement between tongue and lip is often the fault of a worn hinge and cannot be remedied unless the worn joint is replaced.

Solid-gold watch cases are often held together at the joints by a brass pin with solid gold tips to preserve the true gold appearance. Actually, the pin is composed of three sections, the main or brass section and the two gold tips. To simply drive out the pin without a thorough investigation is to invite serious trouble. First, remove the gold tips by using an ordinary square graver and digging in lightly, thereby forcing the tips outward. The brass pin is driven out, the repair work completed, and the pin and tips carefully placed in their original position.

Chapter 11

General Repair

Meaning of metal markings
Repairing scarfpins
Repairing ring mountings with worn filigree work
Sizing an engraved wedding ring
Repairing cuff links
Repairing bracelets
Repairing broken or worn lugs on watchcases
Tightening cameos and similar stones in pins and brooches
Attaching safety chains to bracelets
Repairing costume jewelry

IN THE FIELD of general repair the repairman will work with metals of various qualities. Before entering into details of instruction on the repair of miscellaneous articles of jewelry it would be well to consider first the make-up or the quality of the metals one is likely to encounter. Naturally, one of the first things a jewelry repairman does, before proceeding with a repair, is to look for a stamp, marking, or other indication of what the article is composed of. This is often a determining factor in the method of repair.

Meaning of Metal Markings

Following is a list of markings and their explanation:

E.P.C. Electroplate on copper.
E.P.N.S. Electroplate on nickel silver.
E.P.W.M. Electroplate on white metal.

1/40 12K RGP. One fortieth 12-karat rolled gold plate.

1/20 12K RGP. One twentieth 12-karat rolled gold plate.

Similar markings may be applied to RGF, "rolled gold filled"

R.G.F. Rolled gold filled: the article is composed of a base metal alloy to which a layer or layers of gold plate are joined.

R.G.P. Rolled gold plate: essentially the same as R.G.F., but generally of lower quality.

G.P. Gold plate: the article is composed of base metal on which a plate of gold is deposited by an electroplate process.

10K. Ten-karat gold: the article is 10/24 gold, the other 14/24 being alloy.

12K, 14K, 18K. Twelve-karat gold, fourteen-karat gold, and eighteen-karat gold, or 12/24, 14/24, and 18/24 pure gold, the balance being alloy.

Nickel silver. An alloy that contains about 65% copper, 17½% zinc, and 17½% nickel.

German silver. Another name for *nickel silver*.

Coin silver. An alloy that contains 10% copper and 90% silver.

Sterling silver. An alloy containing 92.5% silver and 7.5% other metal.

Fine silver. 100% pure silver.

10% iridium platinum. The article contains iridium (10%) and platinum (90%).

Rhodium plate. Plated with rhodium (a member of the platinum group of metals) used to plate silverware to prevent tarnish, and on other metals to give a platinum appearance.

Chrome plate. Plated with chromium; usually found on inexpensive articles.

S.S. Stainless steel, used extensively for watch cases and more currently for flatware.

Repairing Scarfpins

Scarfpins usually break at the bend and may be soldered using the electric soldering machine or flame. If the flame is used, lay the broken parts in their correct position on an asbestos pad. Use binding wire to clamp the two parts securely. Apply flux and solder to the joint and proceed to apply the flame. For machine soldering, the mounting may be held with the machine clamp. The stem may be held in a piece of cork while soldering, to keep the heat away from the fingers. The cork is better than soldering tweezers, because the latter may permit the stem to twist or turn during soldering. The tweezers may also mar the stem.

Repairing Ring Mountings with Worn Filigree Work

The worn part may be cut out or filed away entirely. A new flat piece of stock of a thickness equal to the remaining filigree work is fitted into the opening and soldered by flame. This is filed to the shape of the ring. If there is enough clearance for sawing, the filigree work may be replaced by piercing and milgraining the edges. If sawing is impossible, the filigree pattern may be cut out, using a knife-edge graver. This is particular work, and considerable skill is needed. Sometimes the inserted piece is on the underside of the ring, and replacing the filigree is well-nigh impossible. In this case the work may be finished smoothly without the filigree. (The customer should be consulted first.)

Sizing an Engraved Wedding Ring

A wedding ring engraved on the outside may be made smaller quite easily. Saw out the exact amount to reduce the size. Square the ends and bend them together *absolutely flush*. Using the minimum amount of solder, solder the joint by flame or machine. Shape the ring on the mandrel. File the inside and sides flush. Examine the top of the joint, and with a graver trim out excessive solder that has formed next to the milgrained edge. Run the milgrain tool lightly over this section. Buff and finish the ring. The success in doing a nice job here depends on how closely the joint fits before soldering and how small an amount of solder shows after soldering. If the job can be done without showing excessive solder on top, then no trimming is necessary.

A wedding ring engraved on the outside requires a bit of tedious work if it is to be made a size or more larger. The ring is made larger in the usual manner, but the pattern on the ring must be recarved or chased. Special chasing tools must be formed out of steel to match the pattern. The ring is placed on a steel mandrel and the pattern is chased on the ring by tapping the little steel punches. After chasing, the excess metal is cut away from the pattern, setting the pattern in relief. A sharp edge is cut out and milgrained to match the work on the ring. This is advanced work and should not be attempted by a beginner unless he is under the supervision of a competent instructor. A great deal of this work is sent to trade shops specializing in all types of jewelry repairs. This work turns up infrequently because it is possible to buy these engraved rings in almost any size and there is no point in expanding such a ring when the correct size (in a standard pattern) may be ordered and received in a few days.

Repairing Cuff Links

Repairing cuff links depends on the nature of the design. Most joints are hard-soldered. It may be necessary to clamp the job on the asbestos pad and flame-solder. The main difficulty is in holding the work perfectly still in the correct position. Binding wire is used for clamping or wrapping the work in position.

Repairing Bracelets

There are so many different designs it would be impossible to cover all of them. Generally bracelets break at the catch or the joint.

Broken catches are replaced in the following manner:

1. Heat the article until the solder flows and frees the broken catch or broken joint. The broken part is removed with tweezers as the solder loosens its grip.

2. A similar catch or joint is selected from stock. It is inserted or fitted into the receiving slot. If old solder prevents it from entering, the bracelet may be held clamped in the bench vise and heated gradually until the old solder flows and the new part is shoved in position.

Most joints and catches of this nature are soft-soldered, but hard-soldered work may be handled in the same manner.

Other breaks in bracelets are handled as simple soldering jobs and should need no special instruction. Link bracelets may be repaired as explained under Chain Soldering and under Repairing Worn Links or Rings, in Chapter 8.

Quite often snake chain bracelets and others of a similar nature break at the soldered ends where they fit into a slot. It has been the writer's experience that to simply resolder at the break does not give a permanent repair, but one that may break again at any time. A safer job is to remove the broken piece from the groove by heating and melting the solder, then run the broken end into the groove and solder. If the bracelet has two strands, the other must be shortened accordingly. The result using this method is always a slightly shorter bracelet. If more length is desired, the catch adjustment may take care of it or (depending on the design of the bracelet) a link may be added.

Repairing Broken or Worn Lugs on Watchcases

The method depends on the design. If the case is cast and a lug is broken off, it is far better to buy a new case. When lugs break, they usually break at a previous joint that is flush with the case proper. Resoldering is all that is necessary. The main trouble is lining up the lug with the case and the opposite lug. In some instances this may be done with binding wire, clamping the case and the lug to the asbestos pad or charcoal block. In others, all methods to hold the lug in place seem to fail and it becomes necessary to do the job by simply holding the lug with the soldering tweezers, clamping the case lightly but securely in the jaws of the vise. Resting the left hand on the vise and holding the lug in soldering tweezers, apply the flame with the right hand holding the torch. This method may seem very difficult to the beginner, but with considerable practice the technique can be developed and the lug soldered in position at the first attempt. A steady well-braced hand is needed and an eye for alignment. Other similar jobs that ordinarily demand the use of binding wire may be handled in the same manner and to considerable advantage, because the method is a great timesaver. Confidence through much practice is needed, and unless the repairer has this confidence, it is better to continue using binding wire for clamping or wrapping the work.

Repairing or replacing wire lugs on ladies' watches is a comparatively easy job. The wires are sometimes worn through and all that is needed is to replace the worn section with new wire. The wire sometimes breaks away from the case at the solder joint and needs to be resoldered. Occasionally the wire lug is completely worn out and needs replacing. To replace it, select the correct wire first and shape it to the old wire; then remove the old wire and solder the new piece in place. Owing to the central location of the wire lugs, it is better to wrap binding wire around the case and lug to hold it in position. Use a broad blue flame to heat the case and flow the solder. On all case work, do not forget to use the antioxidizing dip before soldering to prevent discoloration. Remember to remove any steel parts before working on the case.

In fitting new wire lugs, the most satisfactory and substantial job can be done by first drilling holes in the case and fitting the wire ends in the holes. On the inside the wire tips may be bent outward and soldered. Low-karat solder, demanding a lower heat, is best for case work.

Wire lugs are rather out of date, but the repairer will get this type of work to do on old watches and on watches that have been converted into strap watches.

Modern ladies' watchcases have a number of different lug arrangements. The usual trouble encountered is not with the lug breaking off, but wearing through. Quite often the lug is made solid with the bezel. The repair would consist of building up the thickness of the worn portion by filling in or inserting a new section.

Tightening Cameos and Similar Stones in Pins and Brooches

Cameos are very fragile and should be handled with utmost care. Large cameos set in pins or brooches are held in place by a bezel which is burnished over the edge of the stone. The larger brooches may be held in the fingers or rested against the bench pin during the tightening operation. To tighten, use a curved-tip burnisher as shown in Fig. 13.46N and explained under Bezel Settings, Chapter 13.

Smaller pins may be cemented firmly on the end of a cement stick and tightened in the same manner. Shellac may be used.

Attaching Safety Chains to Bracelets

Safety chains are usually 2½ to 3 inches long. To attach a safety chain to a bracelet, solder a small jump ring on one side of the catch. Attach the chain to a jump ring of the same size. Solder the jump ring to the bracelet just on the other side of the catch. To the loose end of the chain attach a very small spring ring. The spring ring should fit through the jump ring soldered to the opposite side of the catch. It is best to check the spring ring and jump ring for size before soldering.

Repairing Costume Jewelry

To begin with—what is costume jewelry? We automatically think of the cheapest type of earrings, bracelets, brooches, pins of various styles sold by dime stores, department stores, drugstores, and jewelers. Truly, this is costume jewelry, but the range covered by this term is considerably broader. Many better-class jewelers sell costume jewelry that is far above the lead-base variety, much of it being constructed of a good quality of gold plate. Their interpretation of costume jewelry apparently is derived from the fact that jewelry that is not genuine (not of solid precious metal and consisting of imitation stones) falls in the *costume* category.

This type of jewelry is often just as attractive as a genuine article since it is designed more for eye-catching appeal than for permanent durability. One may well afford several pieces of good costume jewelry as opposed to owning one piece of real or genuine. Hence the popularity of costume jewelry as such.

To repair the cheapest or lead-base variety of costume jewelry is folly, since the cost of repair (if it can be repaired) is usually more than the cost of the article. Too many things can happen during the soldering operation that may spoil the job to risk even beginning such a task. Weigh the advantages and disadvantages.

For example, a customer comes in with a piece of costume jewelry to be repaired, admitting that she paid little for it; but she is so attached to it she can't bear to think of discarding it. This is a cue to win a customer's favor and gratitude, and earn a dollar besides—or is it? Actually one stands about a one-to-five chance of being successful and winning this customer.

Here is what can happen: (1) The peculiar finish, whose process only the manufacturer knows, is destroyed, and although the joint is secured, the beauty is gone. The finish cannot be restored—by the repairer. (2) During the soldering procedure, the lead base of the jewelry melts as soon as the soft solder does, and the area collapses. (3) Frequently these pieces are dipped in a type of lacquer or varnish that turns brown or yellow at the faintest suggestion of heat. Of course it may be possible to remove all this and relacquer; but then how can one afford to spend so much time getting a dollar repair job in order?

The list could go on, but it should now be apparent that the sensible thing to do is sell the customer another article, or suggest the purchase. This cannot damage a reputation. Attempting to repair a doubtful piece of merchandise can.

To repair the better class of costume jewelry requires the use of no new skill other than a careful analysis of the material to be worked with.

To determine whether to soft-solder or hard-solder, use a graver to cut into the broken surface. Soft solder is by nature soft, and will show a bright lead luster; hard solder will offer much resistance to the graver and will be apparent at the first touch. Always solder as the previous joint was soldered.

It is advisable to determine in the beginning just what the material is that needs repairing. If gold-filled or sterling, it will be so marked, and no trouble should be encountered; if, however, there are no markings and the metal is hard, either yellow or white durable metal, then be apprehensive of heat discoloration. The manufacturer is the only one who knows the whole story on the strangely finished metals, and too frequently the finish is very difficult to restore.

In cleaning good costume jewelry, be aware of the artistic shadings and differences in finish that make the item more attractive. Many pieces will have varying degrees of line-finishes in addition to highlights of brightly polished surfaces. Although the task of refinishing such articles is not beyond the average jeweler's ability, the time consumed restoring finishes is very expensive—to the jeweler.

Plenty of foresight before attempting a job seems to be the primary factor to develop. A thorough knowledge of good soldering techniques will serve very well in evaluating jobs that may be too dangerous or unprofitable to repair.

And soldering is only one factor. Refinishing or restoring the item to its original appearance is considerably more of a problem than working with expensive jewelry. Jewelry of better quality is usually of solid metal and can always be restored like new.

Chapter 12

Making Useful Tools

Hardening and tempering steel
Some handy tools to make
Shaping stonesetting gravers

THE TOOLS that a jeweler is required to make are usually quite simple in construction, such as punches, gravers, burnishers, pushers, chasing tools.

Hardening and Tempering Steel

To make good steel tools, bring them to the desired hardness as follows:

FIG. 12.1.   Hardening a tool.
144

1. Cover the tool with a layer of soap.

2. Lay it on an asbestos pad, and with a blue flame, heat until the color is bright cherry red (see Fig. 12.1).

3. Plunge instantly into a pan of clean, cold water, with the tool in a vertical position.

4. Test the hardness by filing the piece. If the piece is glass hard, no impression will be made by the file.

5. Polish the oxidization from the surface, using a medium-grit emery.

6. Proceed to temper. Gradually heat until the desired color is reached. Some tools may be tempered by waving them back and forth through an alcohol flame (Fig. 12.2), closely watching the color change. Other tools may be handled more easily by being placed on a brass plate or pan and heated over a gas flame (Fig. 12.3). If the color change is too rapid, and it is feared that it may go beyond the desired stage, the tool may be submerged in oil or water to arrest the tempering.

The accompanying table shows the colors of heated steel at various temperatures.

Pale straw	420° F
Straw	450° F
Yellow	480° F
Brown	500° F
Purple	550° F
Dark blue	570° F
Light blue	600° F
Blue-green or gray	630° F

In relation to jewelry work, punches and pushers are tempered enough to remove the brittleness that may cause the tool to snap suddenly under strain or stress. The tool should at the same time be hard enough not to bend. A tempering color of yellow or brown is satisfactory. Gravers used in stonesetting must be very hard and yet have enough resiliency to prevent the point from breaking. They should be tempered to a light straw color. Tempering hard steel strengthens and toughens the metal even though it is made somewhat softer.

Some Handy Tools to Make

1. *Prong or claw tightener:* From steel stock, select a rod measuring 2.5 mm in diameter. File and shape as shown in Fig. 12.4A. The end of the tool must be filed absolutely flat. Harden, draw to a straw color, and drive the rod into a handle already prepared to

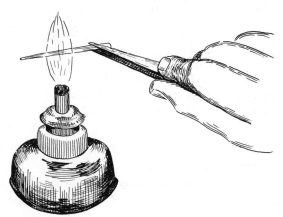

FIG. 12.2.   Tempering a tool in an alcohol flame.

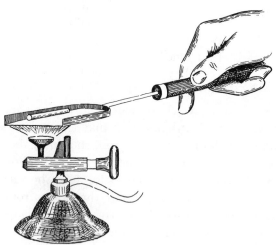

FIG. 12.3.   Tempering a tool over a gas flame.

receive it (Fig. 12.4B). This tool should not exceed $3\frac{3}{4}$ inches in length, and the face should not be highly polished.

2. *Prong pusher or bender for setting and tightening stones:* From steel stock measuring 3 mm square, saw a $2\frac{1}{2}$-inch length. File to the shape shown in Fig. 12.5A. The edges must be straight. The tapered end will be driven into a graver handle that has been drilled to receive it (Fig. 12.5B). The other end is filed, showing two faces. Note that these faces are filed at different angles.

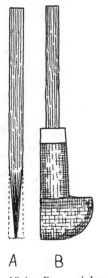

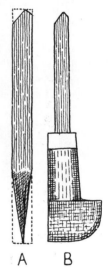

FIG. 12.4.   Prong tightener.   FIG. 12.5.   Prong pusher.

Harden the piece, draw it to a dark straw color, and drive it into the handle.

Rough file marks should not be left on the faces. They should be polished sufficiently to remove all file marks, but here again no bright polish is wanted.

3. *A tool useful for very small settings:* From steel stock measuring 2 mm square, saw a $2\frac{1}{2}$-inch length. File and shape exactly as the tool just completed in Fig. 12.5. The over-all length of each of the two tools should not exceed $3\frac{3}{4}$ inches.

4. *Stone tighteners or bezel-closing punches:* From steel stock measuring 3 mm square, saw four 3-inch lengths (see Fig. 12.6). File and shape them until the tips measure (A) .75 × 2 mm; (B) .5 × 1.5 mm; (C) 1 mm square; and (D) .75 mm square.

Harden and draw each piece to a straw color. The tips should be filed straight, leaving no rounded edges. Do not bright-polish the tips.

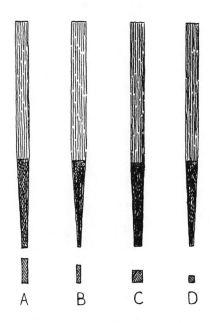

Fig. 12.6.   Stone tighteners.

A   B   C   D

5. *Tool for tightening insignia:* Select a piece of drill rod measuring 3¾ inches in length (Fig. 12.7A) and 2.55 mm in diameter. Grind the end to fit into the wooden handle (Fig. 12.7B). Shape the opposite end to a short taper, the sides forming a right angle. This taper may be finished with a #00 emery stick, and then the tip must be heated and bent about ¼ inch from the point of the tool (Fig. 12.7C). The bending may be done after driving the tool into the handle. To make the bend, hold the tool by the handle in the right hand and place the tip diagonally on a hard asbestos pad. With the left hand apply the heat from the torch to the desired

area and pressing with the right hand allow the tool to bend upward until a right angle is reached. A second bend is necessary, starting 1 inch from the bend just made. Apply the flame and bend in the same manner until the shape shown in Fig. 12.7C is reached. The tool is now ready for hardening and tempering. Remove the tool from the handle and proceed as explained above, Hardening and Tempering Steel. Draw the temper to a dark straw color. The tool must not be brittle nor soft enough to bend under pressure.

The completed tool is now ready to use in tightening emblems

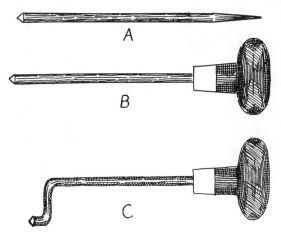

FIG. 12.7.   Tools for tightening insignia.

or insignia that are fitted over stones by means of a pipe or pipes running through the stone. The pipe is "lipped" over the stone on the underside, thus holding itself secure. Sometimes the stone has a prepared countersink to receive this lip. In tightening, the shield or insignia may be rested against the bench block; the tip of the tool is placed in the hole in the pipe, and with a circular motion the metal is burnished, thereby being pressed to the stone and becoming tight. This must be done very carefully, for there is always great danger of cracking the stone.

6. *Punch for driving out rivets in bar pins and brooches:* Select a piece of drill rod measuring 2 mm in diameter and 2¼ inches in

length. Roll-file the piece to a gradual taper measuring .75 mm at the tip. Fig. 12.8A shows the rod before roll-filing and two alternative ways of shaping the tip (Fig. 12.8B, C). As this punch is used in driving out rivets in bar pins and brooches, a long taper is unnecessary. Harden the tool and draw the temper to a dark straw color.

7. *Three tapered pin pushers:* Select three pieces of drill rod. The first pusher should measure 2½ inches in length and taper

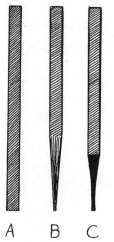
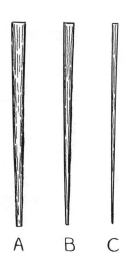

A   B   C   A   B   C

Fig. 12.8. Punch for driving out   Fig. 12.9.   Pin pushers.
rivets.

from 1.25 mm to .75 mm; the second, 2 inches in length, taper from 1.0 mm to .55 mm; the third, 1½ inches in length, taper from 6 mm to 3 mm. Great care must be exercised here in order to obtain a gradual taper from tip to tip. A finer finish is desired on these punches or pin pushers. After using the finest file, they may be polished with a fine-grit emery stick. To prevent bending, the three pin pushers should be hardened and tempered to a dark straw color. These tapered tools are used as punches or pushers in removing hinge pins from lockets, watchcases, compacts, or any jewelry so constructed. They may be used to advantage by placing the large end in a pin vise, thus creating a longer and more easily handled tool. A stubborn pin may be removed by lightly tapping the pin pusher or the end of the pin vise.

Fig. 12.9A, B, C shows the correctly shaped pin pushers and their comparative sizes.

Shaping Stonesetting Gravers

To sharpen a graver accurately, place an oilstone, the graver, the graver sharpener (Fig. 12.11), and flat section of plate glass as shown in Fig. 12.12A. The graver sharpener will hold the graver firmly after the correct adjustment is made for the belly angle or face angle. The base of the graver sharpener is moved back and forth across the section of plate glass as the tip of the graver moves

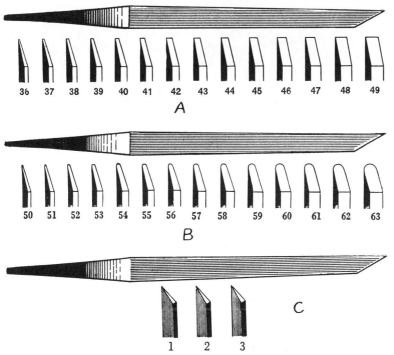

FIG. 12.10.   Gravers: *A*, flat; *B*, round; *C*, knife-edge.

across the stone. The stone and section of plate glass should be placed on the same level and remain in position until the end of the sharpening operation. To move the position of the stone or the glass after beginning to sharpen would change the angle slightly and cause the surface being ground to become rounded.

Many stonesetters never use a graver sharpener but prefer to sharpen by hand, finding this method quite a timesaver during a busy day. To sharpen by hand requires a degree of skill that comes only with experience. It is suggested that the beginner not concern himself with hand sharpening until he has a thorough understanding of how his gravers should be shaped. It is far better to

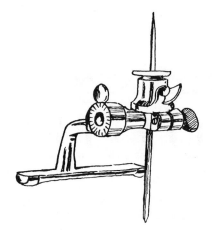

Fig. 12.11.   Graver sharpener.

learn to set stones with correctly sharpened gravers. Then after the setting skill is acquired, one may consider the advantages or disadvantages of sharpening by hand.

Graver for trimming settings: Select a #40 flat tool (see Fig. 12.12B) and a graver handle (Fig. 12.13). Drill the graver handle to receive the graver. All gravers are too long when bought and must be shortened. The completed tool should measure 3½ to 4 inches in length. The graver end may be broken off and ground to a taper so that when driven into the handle there is little danger of splitting. Be sure to reduce the length from the handle end, not the other end.

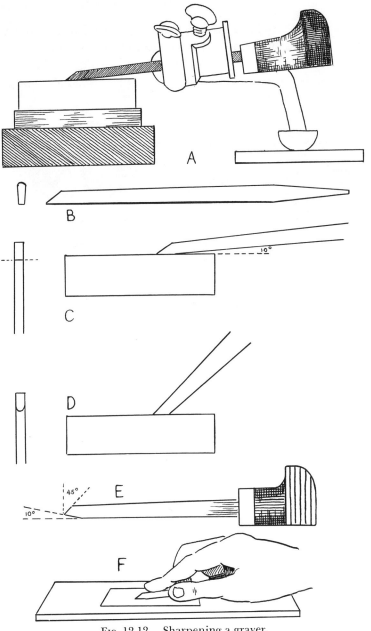

Fig. 12.12.   Sharpening a graver.

Sharpen the belly first, by grinding a perfectly flat face, noticing the rear line, not the tip of the tool to determine straightness. A belly angle of 10° is generally satisfactory (see Fig. 12.12C). This angle depends greatly on the individual. The 10° angle will serve

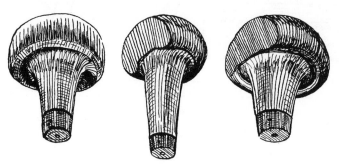

Fig. 12.13.   Graver handles.

as a guide. A short belly is more desirable. Grind first on the India oilstone (Fig. 12.14A), then on the Arkansas stone (Fig. 12.14B) and polish by hand, using 4-0 emery paper placed over glass. A high polish is desired (see Fig. 12.12F). Now grind the face to a 45° angle with the edge perfectly straight (Fig. 12.12D). The face need not be as highly polished as the belly. Care should be taken

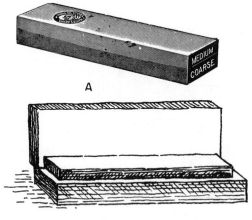

Fig. 12.14.   Oilstones: *A*, India oilstone; *B*, Arkansas oilstone.

to see that no burrs remain after polishing on the Arkansas stone. Stabbing the graver in a firm piece of wood will remove burrs. One or two polishing strokes on 4-0 emery are sufficient. It is well to remember that overpolishing may round edges. This graver is used for trimming settings.

The round graver: Select a #52 round tool. Reduce the length as explained and mount the tool in the handle. Since the belly is already properly shaped (Fig. 12.15A), it only remains to grind the face. The face is ground to an angle of about 60° to 65° and finished the same as the flat tool (Fig. 12.15B, C). The belly may be polished slightly on 4-0 emery, with a rolling motion. This is to ensure a sharp edge and the removal of all burrs. The round graver will be used in shaping beads in stonesetting.

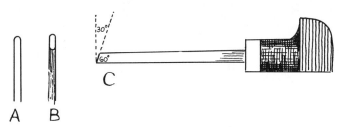

FIG. 12.15.   Shaping a round graver.

The onglet graver: This graver is shortened in the same manner as the flat graver. The sharpening is quite different and can best be understood by studying Fig. 12.16. Fig. 12.16A shows the belly, which is not altered. It may be polished on emery paper to improve the edge. Fig. 12.16B shows the face after sharpening. To arrive at this shape the graver must be tilted to the side as shown in Fig. 12.16D. The face is ground on the India stone, and then on the Arkansas stone and slightly polished on emery.

The knife-edge graver: This graver is shortened to the usual 3½- to 4-inch length. It is sharpened by grinding a 45° face angle, using India and Arkansas stone (Fig. 12.17B and C). Slightly polish with emery paper. The belly (Fig. 12.17A) is sharpened on the Arkansas stone by hand, rubbing one side and then the other in much the same manner as sharpening a knife or whetting a razor (Fig. 12.17D). A sharp edge is desired. Polish with 4-0 emery. Avoid a featheredge or one ground too thin. This tool is used in forming beads in stonesetting.

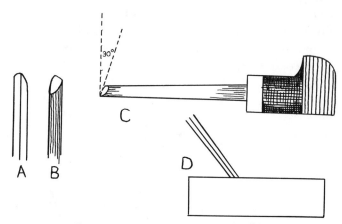

FIG. 12.16.   Shaping an onglet graver.

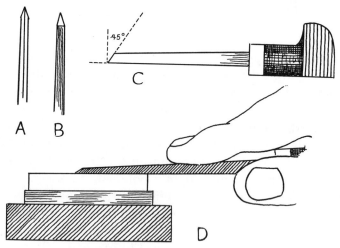

FIG. 12.17.   Shaping a knife-edge graver.

Chapter 13

Stonesetting

ALTHOUGH a successful stonesetter is not required to be a gemologist in the true sense of the word, it is nevertheless very important that he avail himself of certain fundamental knowledge that might affect decisions in setting certain stones. It is suggested that one who intends to devote much of his time to setting stones should acquire reference books dealing specifically with the subject. Trade journals may also be counted on to hold a wealth of information, most of it especially valuable for keeping one abreast of current trends and developments.

Although the term *stonesetting* might literally mean the setting of all types of stones, the average jewelry-store technician (watchmaker, jeweler, engraver combination man) or the jeweler stonesetter is primarily interested in the setting of diamonds. The following instruction procedures will endeavor to explain and illustrate in detail the most important styles and methods of diamond setting.

Speaking very generally, diamonds are graded by style of cutting, color, and imperfections. The style of cutting shows the stone to its best advantage. The color may contain slight yellow, brown, or blue tints. There may be an absence of all tints. Slight imperfections such as carbon spots or inclusions devaluate considerably an otherwise perfect stone.

Fig. 13.1A shows a large-scale drawing of a brilliant-cut diamond which has 58 facets altogether. The outer edge shown at G and G' is the *girdle*. The portion above G and G' is considered the *crown*. The flat top or T–T' is the *table*. The portion below, G–G', is the

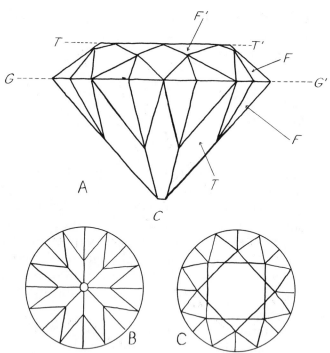

Fig. 13.1.   Brilliant-cut diamond: *A*, side view; *B*, pavilion; *C*, crown.

pavilion. The small flat face at *C* is the *culet.* The sides and faces that reflect the brilliance are called *facets,* shown at *F.* Fig. 13.1B shows the pavilion of a brilliant-cut stone. Fig. 13.1C shows the crown of a brilliant-cut stone.

The table on hardness of precious stones is based on the diamond which is rated at 10 in hardness.

Tiffany Mountings

The Tiffany mounting represents one of the oldest techniques in setting stones and will be presented first in the following series of basic setting styles. It is suggested that the beginner carefully study the construction of the Tiffany mounting and at the same time examine a finished Tiffany diamond ring set with a stone of at least one-half carat. This is to get a clear picture of what must be accomplished and to formulate the correct concept of what stone-setting really is.

Although the professionally finished Tiffany diamond ring may appear to require an exceptionally refined technique in the setting of the diamond, the finished product is actually composed of a series of relatively simple operations. The results of these individual operations can be seen progressively in Figure 13.2.

At a glance it is apparent that setting a diamond in a Tiffany mounting is merely burring out metal (or removing metal) inside the six prongs to form a seat for the stone. Then, the tips of the prongs are weakened (by filing) and gradually pushed over the girdle of the diamond, thus holding it securely.

When setting a diamond for the first time it is quite a difficult thing to overcome the fear of ruining the head or damaging the stone in some way. However, it does not take many completed stonesetting jobs to increase confidence and become easy with the work. A diamond well set is a thing of beauty, a work of art, and a great satisfaction to the stonesetter.

These are the tools necessary for setting a diamond in a Tiffany mounting: a set of conventional diamond setting burrs, 2 prong pushers, a caliper gauge, a #40 or #42 flat graver, a small barrette file, beeswax, and a flexible shaft machine.

More equipment is needed for the other types of mountings, but here we will discuss only the tools related to the Tiffany mounting. The diamond-setting burrs are of the conventional type, available from any jewelers' supply house, and should be purchased as a complete set, that is, all the available sizes of burrs as seen in Fig. 13.3.

The barrette file (small jeweler's file) must be prepared for filing directly over the stone without any risk of damage. The edges are ground smooth by rubbing back and forth over the India stone and then the Arkansas stone. After this operation, examine for rough areas by sliding the edge over the end of the fingernail. This file will be used in shaping the tips of the prongs after the pushing operation is completed.

COMPARATIVE HARDNESS OF STONES
(Diamond = 10)

Diamond	10
Ruby	9
Emerald	9
Sapphire	9
Topaz	8
Garnet	5 to 8
Amethyst	7
Turquoise	6
Opal	5½ to 6

Beeswax is used merely to lift the stone in and out of the mounting head during the setting operation. The wax may be pressed into any shape; the shape illustrated in Fig. 13.4 is suggested as the most desirable.

We are now ready to begin setting the diamond. Fig. 13.2G and H shows the finished product, and it would be well to study the figure carefully before beginning any work. Note that the girdle fits snugly into the prongs, and that there is no gap or space showing between the stone and the metal prongs.

1. Select the correct mounting (Fig. 13.2A). To do this, place

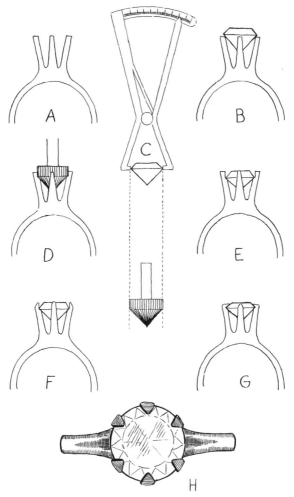

Fig. 13.2.   Steps in a Tiffany mounting.

the stone directly over the six prongs. The stone should cover one-third of each tip, leaving two-thirds showing (Fig. 13.2B). Prongs

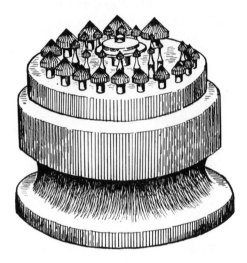

FIG. 13.3.   Bearing burrs.

can be spread inward or outward slightly, using small snipe-nose pliers.

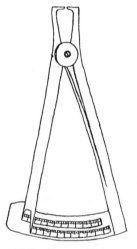

FIG. 13.4.   Using beeswax to lift the stone.

FIG. 13.5.   Degree ligne gauge.

2. Select the correct burr (Fig. 13.3). Using a stone gauge (Fig. 13.5), measure the stone at the girdle (Fig. 13.2C). Select a burr with the same measurement or very slightly smaller. When used, the burr will make a seat slightly larger than its actual measure.

3. Holding the mounting in the ring clamp, insert the burr in the flexible-shaft chuck and with a medium speed, sink the burr to

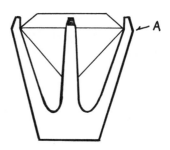

FIG. 13.6.   Filing the prong tips.

the depth shown in Fig. 13.2D. Too high a speed may cause excessive vibration and enlarge the seat, too slow a speed may bend the prongs and chatter.

A high crown indicates a longer prong. A shallow crown will be safe with a shorter prong. Never use excessively long or bulky prongs on any crown for they will detract from the stone. Be very sure the stone rests equally on all six prongs.

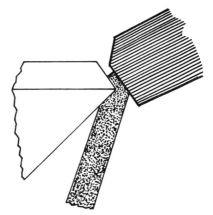

FIG. 13.7.   Using a two-sided pusher.

4. With a small file or flat graver, remove from the sides of each prong the metal burr caused by burring the seat.

5. Using the small barrette file, remove some of the metal from the prong tips and prepare them for bending and pushing over the girdle. Note at Fig. 13.2F that the thickness of the prong at the greatest point of wear is not reduced by the filing. Only the tip is weakened. See Fig. 13.6 (an enlargement of Fig. 13.2F) for the filing method.

6. To begin the bending operation use snipe-nose pliers as illustrated in Fig. 14.4. This changes the angle or direction of the

Fig. 13.8.	Bending the tips.

"push" and minimizes pressure against the stone. The direction of "push" may now be parallel with the side of the crown, or nearly so.

7. Place the stone in the seat and continue to bend prongs with the two-sided pusher first (Fig. 13.7), and then with the round pusher (Fig. 13.8). Always work on opposite prongs, gradually tightening until the stone is firm and level. If the tips do not bend easily, file away a little metal until they do. Leave each tip as heavy

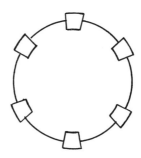

FIG. 13.9. All the prongs in position against crown.

as possible at the bend, for it receives more wear at this point. Finally, the round pusher may be used at the very tip, pressing downward and closing any gaps that may exist between the metal and the stone. The result of all this manipulation may look like Fig. 13.9.

8. The trimming and polishing operation follows this step and the barrette file may be used directly against the stone since it has been prepared for this particular operation (smoothed at the edges). The prong tips are shaped to a rounded point to avoid pulling threads from clothing or stockings. Fig. 13.10 shows an enlarged view of a prong indicating facets or planes created by

FIG. 13.10. Finished prongs.

filing. The sharp edges will later be rounded slightly as polishing continues. The final result is seen in Fig. 13.2G. Another way to trim is by using a highly polished flat tool to bright-cut and shape the tips. Care must be taken not to scratch a soft stone.

9. Check all tips for burrs and remove with a flat graver any burrs found. A light touch is all that is necessary to cut off these burrs. In shaping the tips with the file, sharp edges will result. These should not be left. However, when file marks and scratches are buffed out, these edges usually round themselves slightly, and a well-shaped tip results that is not sharp enough to endanger clothing.

10. Remove all file marks by buffing. A stiff bristle brush is best for this work. If file marks are not deep, red rouge alone may remove them. If file marks are deep on the outside of the tip, they may be hand-buffed with emery and then machine-buffed with rouge. Check the setting job for burrs before applying it to a soft, finishing cloth buff.

11. Wash in the cleaning solution.

12. Dip in alcohol and allow to dry.

13. Check the job again to be sure that the stone is tight and that no burrs remain.

To become thoroughly adept at setting the Tiffany, the beginner is advised to use large glass stones, about the equivalent size of a carat diamond, gradually reducing the size to a $1/4$-carat stone. During this practice work it is well to remember that working with glass stones is considerably more difficult than working with diamonds. The diamond will withstand much more abuse than the glass counterpart, for the slightest amount of excess pressure will crack the glass stone and the slightest error with a file will scratch it. To complete the setting of a glass stone without a blemish is an accomplishment to be proud of and certainly qualifies the setter to work with a diamond.

Flat-Top Mountings

Of all the different styles of mountings, skill in setting a stone in the flat-top is the most difficult to develop. This is because so many operations must be executed flawlessly, each one requiring different tools and methods.

Due to the complications, the methods will be discussed in two sections. The first section will explain and illustrate the basic operations step-by-step so that the order of setting the stone may be understood. The second section will deal with the individual operations separately, showing enlarged views and explaining how to use the round graver in bead forming, the flat graver in trimming away excess metal, and the milgrain tool for the final embellishment.

Sequence of Operations

1. Select the right size of burr, as explained above, Tiffany Mountings.

2. Sink the burr, using the ring clamp to hold the mounting (Fig. 13.11A) and the flexible-shaft chuck to hold the burr (Fig. 13.11B). The stone should fit snugly with little or no side play (Fig. 13.11C).

3. With the stone out of the seat, use a knife-edge graver to begin trimming out a bead.

4. With the round graver start a cut as shown in Fig. 13.11F. This is done by rocking the tool from side to side, not by pushing forward. As the cut increases in depth, the tip of the bead being formed is gradually pushed in the direction of the space to be occupied by the stone, which as yet has not been placed in the mounting. The shape of the tool is pushing the bead. It is not necessary to push forward at all. Make similar cuts at all four corners.

5. Place the stone in position. Work from opposite corners so that the stone remains level. Deepen the cuts (Fig. 13.11G).

6. When the stone is secure, the rounding and final tightening is done with a beading tool (Figs. 13.11H and 13.11I).

7. With a #38, #40, or #42 flat tool, depending on the width of cut desired, trim out the metal between the girdle and the outer edge of the flat top in the manner shown in Fig. 13.12A.

8. As the trimming is completed to the side of the flat top, a

sharp line should result as straight as a knife edge (Fig. 13.12B). Over this edge is run a milgrain tool which forms a series of tiny beads (Fig. 13.12C). This tool has a wheel at the tip. This is fitted over the edge (Fig. 13.12D). Fig. 13.12E shows the final result.

9. The setting job may now be buffed if it appears necessary. It is quite possible to obtain a setting and trimming job that needs no buffing. It is permissible to buff the finished job lightly with a soft bristle brush or a cloth buff.

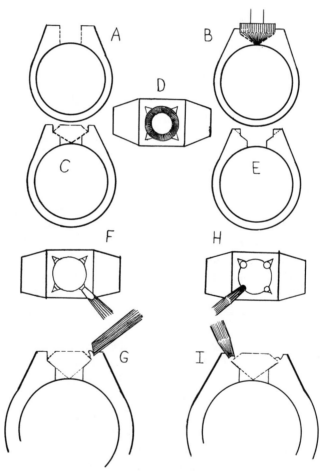

FIG. 13.11.   Steps in the flat-top mounting.

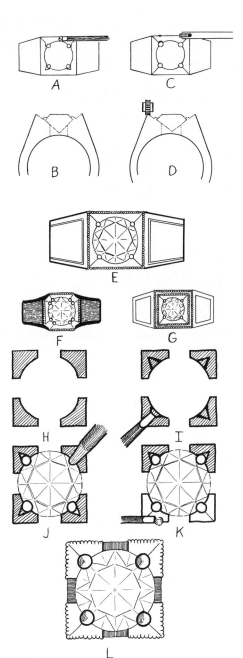

Fig. 13.12. Finishing
the flat-top mounting.

10. Wash the ring in the cleaning solution.

11. Dip in alcohol and allow to dry.

Bead Forming, Trimming, and Milgraining

Fig. 13.13 shows a direct view of a diamond in a flat-top setting —without milgraining.

Fig. 13.14 shows the beginning V cut used to isolate the bead before using the round graver. This cut is executed with a knife-edge graver or round graver.

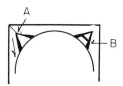

Fig. 13.13. The completed setting operations.

Fig. 13.14. Preliminary cuts for bead forming: *A*, beginning cut with knife-edge graver; *B*, beginning cut with round graver.

Fig. 13.15A shows the method of holding the #52 round graver prior to the bead raising operation.

And, speaking of bead raising, the term is misleading as the next few illustrations will prove. What actually happens is the forcing of a bit of metal downward and over the edge of the diamond's girdle. The trimming away of the surplus metal gives the finished bead a raised appearance.

The #52 round graver is shaped bluntly, as shown in the side view, Fig. 13.16. To begin "raising" the bead, the tip of the graver is placed in the position shown in Fig. 13.15B. The tool is rocked from side to side to start the cut. Then, using the same rocking motion, the position of the graver is elevated as shown in Fig. 13.16. Fig. 13.17 shows the final position of the round graver with the bead pressed flush to the stone. One point to remember in using the round graver—the shape of the blunt face automatically pushes the bead over the edge of the girdle as the point is forced deeper into the metal.

The next step is to shape the bead, using the beading tool as shown in Figs. 13.18 and 13.19. This operation presses the bead

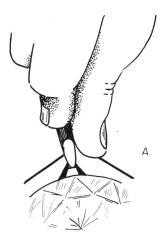

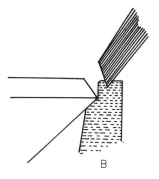

FIG. 13.15. Bead raising: *A*, position for forming bead using a round graver; *B*, side view of beginning cut using round graver.

even more firmly against the stone, at the same time shaping and polishing the metal.

The remaining procedures are all trimming and shaping operations and will receive the greatest emphasis, since it is here that beginners usually get "bogged down."

Using a #40 flat graver, begin to trim as shown in Fig. 13.20. This must be very carefully controlled, for a slip could easily remove the bead and possibly damage the edge of the stone. A great deal of practice is necessary with the flat graver to acquire perfect control of the tool. Fig. 13.21 shows the metal removed.

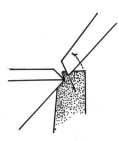

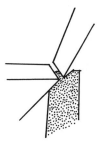

Fig. 13.16. Direction of force used in bending bead toward stone.

Fig. 13.17. Final position as bead touches stone.

See Figs. 13.22 and 13.23 for the position used for trimming the sides. Figs. 13.24 and 13.25 show the metal removed. Always remember to make many light, shallow cuts in trimming away metal, rather than deep cuts.

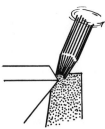

Fig. 13.18. Position of beading tool, beginning at base.

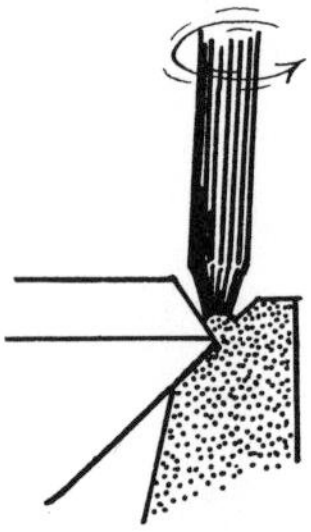

Fig. 13.19. Position of beading tool as beading is completed.

Fig. 13.20. Beginning trim cut toward bead.

Fig. 13.26 shows the position used for removing metal in the far corner. The illustration indicates a forward cut that could mar the bead or possibly cut it away. This is always a risk, and skill in

FIG. 13.21.   Result of beginning cut.

controlling the graver must be developed to prevent such accidents. An aid to reducing the possibility of accidents is shown in Fig. 13.38. A flat graver is prepared to parallel with the corner line

FIG. 13.22.   Beginning side cuts.

FIG. 13.23.   Result of first cut on side.

leading to the bead. Fig. 13.27 shows the appearance after metal is removed.

The final corner trim cuts shown in Figs. 13.28, 13.29, and 13.30 reveal the final results of the cuts.

FIG. 13.24.   Continuing to trim the side.

FIG. 13.25.   Result of continued trimming.

At this point, particularly, the condition of the graver should be restored to a sharp edge and a bright polish. The final cuts on this area should leave a bright luster so that polishing on the lathe is unnecessary. This may sound difficult, but it is certainly a desired effect.

FIG. 13.26. Trimming out the far corner.

FIG. 13.27. Result of primary trimwork on first side of flat-top.

Buffing settings will always round edges no matter how lightly they are touched to the buff. A master stonesetter can trim out his settings so that buffing them would detract from the appearance

FIG. 13.28. Trimming to the right of the bead.

FIG. 13.29. Trimming to the left of the bead.

FIG. 13.30. The completed side.

rather than enhance it. A highly polished graver will leave a bright cut, and smooth cuts will leave a perfectly flat surface.

On the larger stones, it is often desirable to use a triple bead cluster in each corner rather than the conventional single bead. See Fig. 13.31. Two beads do the work of holding the stone; the third is merely ornamental.

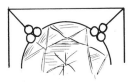

FIG. 13.31. Using three beads to a corner.

If a double row of milgraining is wanted, a knife-edge graver may be used, as shown in Fig. 13.32, to form two sharp edges. Fig. 13.33 shows a cross-section view—the arrow at *A* shows the groove cut by the graver; the arrow at *B* shows the beveled edge formed by a jeweler's barrette file.

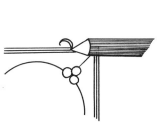

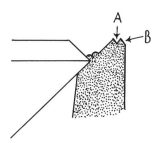

FIG. 13.32. Forming track for milgrain tool using knife-edge graver.

FIG. 13.33. Cross-section of cut made with knife-edge graver.

In Fig. 13.34 we see the milgrain tool following the sharp edges. The tool is held firmly to avoid slipping and is carefully moved back and forth over the edge or track. Caution—this operation should not be overdone. First, advance the tool along the track for a short distance, then reverse the motion or back track. Advance the tool a little farther and back track again slightly. By advancing the tool a little farther each time, a clean, sharp row of milgraining will result. To overwork the edges will cause a flattened, undefined row of indentations little resembling a thin row of beads.

Exercises in Bead Forming

Since skill must be developed in bead forming before the beginner is qualified to attempt work on the precious metals, practice rings with flat tops soldered in position may be formed out of brass stock. The idea is to form beads, hundreds of them, until complete confidence is attained.

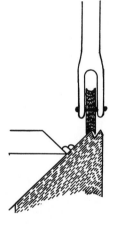

FIG. 13.34. Engaging the milgrain tool to the track or edge.

In making up these practice articles, there is no need to be concerned with anything beyond the surface that will be worked on. For the construction of a simulated ring and flat top, see Fig. 13.35A, B, and C. This may be a section of brass, copper, or nickel about 1½ mm thick. It is sawed out of plate stock in 4, 5, or 6 mm squares. These squares are soldered to the ring shank at Fig. 13.35B. A hole is drilled in the exact center; the flat top is smoothed out using a medium-coarse emery stick, then polished with a medium-fine emery stick.

Before beginning to form beads, see Figs. 13.36 and 13.37. In Fig. 13.36 the area is marked off to accommodate 15 or 20 beads, and the cutting with the knife-edge graver is begun. In Fig. 13.37

beads are formed, as previously explained, thus using up the entire area of usable metal.

Note that no stone is indicated in the illustration. The first attempts should be made without the use of a stone. This exercise is directed toward the forming of the bead only, and all imaginable errors may be made until familiarity with metal resistance is gained. When a degree of bead control is reached, an attempt at setting using a new top may be made: try to form beads that contact the stone and hold it firmly without marring it. When the

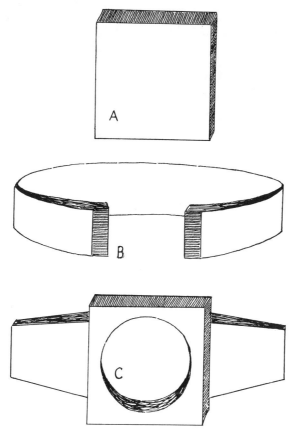

Fig. 13.35. Constructing a practice flat-top mounting.

skill to set glass stones level and unmarred has been attained, the beginner is ready to set diamonds in precious metals. In actual practice, the diamond is less subject to damage than is the glass imitation.

Fig. 13.36. Pattern of cuts before raising beads.

Fig. 13.37. Completed practice beads.

Exercises in Trimming

Beginning with fresh practice rings, set glass stones, beginning with one-carat size and reducing to ¼-carat size as skill increases. Use one bead in each corner and then concentrate on learning to develop skill in trimming using the flat graver. One should use cutting or trimming strokes as long as possible, keeping in mind that many different planes are created with short strokes. The perfect situation is to have only one plane visible, as though the trimming were done in one stroke. This is practically impossible, but it is possible to simulate the appearance of it with carefully executed long, shallow strokes near the end of the trimming operation.

After successfully beading and trimming practice rings, the edges may be milgrained as an additional exercise.

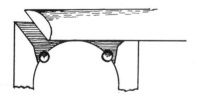

Fig. 13.38. Using flat graver shaped to conform to corner.

While the complete trimming job may be done using the conventionally sharpened flat graver, an aid to trimming in the corners is shown in Fig. 13.38. In this illustration the face of the flat graver is altered to conform to the corner line running from the outer edge to the bead, thus eliminating some of the awkward positions in trimming the corners with the conventional flat gravers.

Fishtail Mountings

The fishtail mounting is one of the most popular of the current styles, being very delicate and artistic in appearance (Fig. 13.39A, B). It has the added advantage of displaying the stone in a most flattering manner, making small stones appear larger and large stones more beautiful. Very little of the stone is covered by metal; all that is necessary to hold it secure is the tiny tip of the fishtail design. These tips must be set neatly, precisely, and with great care; the slightest error, such as a stone not level or a claw too large or too small, is easily detected without a loupe, and most certainly by the critical customer who is purchasing the ring or mounting, as the case may be.

Owing to the construction of the fishtail mounting, slight expansion or shrinking is possible. If the stone to be set is a shade too large for the mounting, it is possible to spread the four corners outward by bending with smooth-jaw (snipe-nose) pliers. The procedure should never be carried to the point of distortion. It is better to delay the job and order a mounting of the correct size, one that will fit without plier manipulation. It is always possible to mar, nick, or flatten the artistic designs at the corners while bending them. It would appear best to consider all these possibilities before deciding to expand or shrink any mounting.

For the beginner, the best thing on which to practice is the real head of a mounting. This can be purchased from findings manufacturers or jewelry supply houses, and although it may seem expensive for practice work, there is no substitute or improvisation that would be less expensive in time spent to make it. Actually, three heads should be enough for one who is familiar with tools,

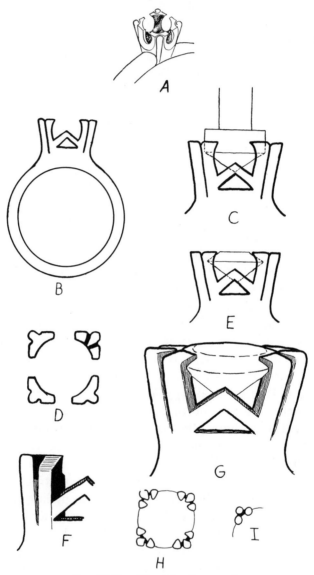

FIG. 13.39.   The fishtail mounting.

and the cost involved in learning such a valuable operation seems comparatively slight.

For practice, solder a white-gold head to a yellow shank, one that will take a ¾-carat diamond. Select a glass stone and prepare to set it. It is comforting to know that anyone who can correctly set a glass stone in a fishtail mounting should have no trouble at all with a real diamond. Diamonds will stand far more punishment than ordinary glass. The setting procedure, by steps, is as follows:

1. Check the stone and mounting for size. To do this, place the diamond in position on top of the head. With the eyes directly over the mounting, held in a ring clamp, it is easy to see how much metal will remain. This will govern the decision as to how the claws (or prongs) will be formed. If the amount of metal remaining is great, a heavy, triangular prong is best (see Fig. 13.39H). If the remaining metal is scant, it is advisable to leave as much as possible, by not filing but shaping the prong in a rounded-bead fashion (Fig. 13.39I). It is very easy to shape the tip of a prong with a beading tool by simply removing the little burrs that normally occur during the procedure. The beading tool serves especially well to press the tip firmly against the stone. For the heavier triangular prongs a pusher is used.

2. Sink the burr as previously explained (Fig. 13.39C).

3. With a thin jeweler's-saw blade, make two cuts, one in each corner (Fig. 13.39D). The depth of the cut should equal the depth of the seat of the stone, or where the girdle will rest (Fig. 13.39E). Now three islands of metal will be observed; one will be a protective prong, the other two will be the "duty" prongs—holding the stone.

4. File the tips of the two outside claws preparatory to bending them over as explained above, Tiffany Mountings. Be sure to file parallel to the girdle of the stone (Fig. 13.39F). After the sawing and filing operations, some chance burrs may have collected around the seat, and it may be necessary to clean these out by using the original setting burr with a very light touch.

5. Place the stone in position, and with a prong pusher bend opposite prongs over until the stone is tight and level (Fig. 13.40). To do this successfully, gradually push the tip in a half-pushing, half-burnishing manner, using the long side of the pusher tip. As it begins to bend, change immediately to the opposite prong,

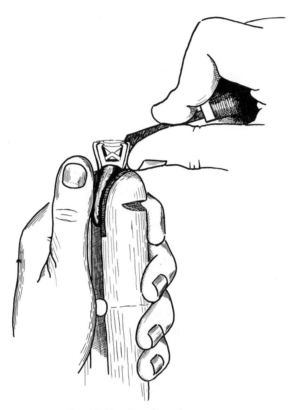

FIG. 13.40.   Bending the prongs.

working it over equally as much as the first prong. It is very important to proceed gradually, always pushing a little at a time, continually shifting corners until the stone reaches a degree of firmness. This careful procedure is to prevent any possibility of the stone getting off level. When the stone has become fairly firm, continue to tighten completely by using the short side of the prong pusher. The flat-tipped round pusher is also helpful at this point.

6. The prongs may be left square (Fig. 13.39G) or slightly pointed in shape (Fig. 13.39H). If the prongs are left square, burnish the tips or edges closest to the stone with a back-and-forth motion parallel to the edge of the stone. This will produce a slight beveled effect that is pleasing in appearance and insures close contact with the stone.

7. To finish and polish the job, use a very fine barrette file to remove all rough spots on the prongs. Do not attempt to file the prongs in a rounded fashion. In the final polishing operation the surfaces and edges will become slightly rounded anyway, but the original definite shape of each prong should be preserved. No definite point is desired as shown in setting Tiffany mountings. All that is necessary is a well-shaped claw as illustrated.

Check the entire setting job for minute burrs and eliminate them. It is sometimes necessary to use a graver to cut them off, since the burrs may be hugging the stone flatly and a file will not always remove them. There is a further use for a graver: it is sometimes necessary to clean out the saw grooves with a thin flat graver (#36) in order to attain the desired crisp professional appearance. A graver will leave a smooth, bright finish with one cut.

Using a bristle wheel brush charged with rouge, bring each prong as well as the entire head to a bright polish. For a finishing touch, lightly apply a flannel wheel buff without the addition of rouge.

8. Wash in the cleaning solution.

9. Dip in alcohol and dry in sawdust.

Illusion-Type Mountings

See Fig. 13.41A and B for a beginning view of an illusion-type mounting. Such a mounting varies from the fundamental designs previously discussed in two distinct ways. First, the bead section is raised and partially shaped, waiting only to be pushed over the edge of the girdle (after seating). The other feature is the ring of metal surrounding the stone after the setting is completed. This

type of setting is intended to flatter the size of any stone, making
a small stone appear larger and more brilliant.

After a seat is burred out for the stone (Fig. 13.41C) the beads
are worked over the edge of the girdle as shown in Fig. 13.41D.
First use the round graver, #51 or #52. Place it far enough back
of the raised bead section to insure an adequate bead. By wiggling
the tool from side to side (Fig. 13.41D, 1) the metal automatically
curls over the edge of the girdle. Fig. 13.41D, 2, shows the beading

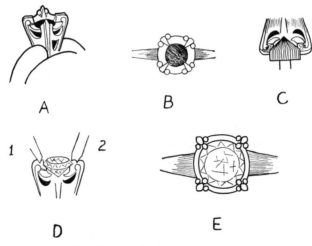

FIG. 13.41.   Illusion-type mounting.

tool shaping the bead and pressing it firmly against the stone. It is
wise, of course, to work from one corner to the opposite corner
so that the stone may be kept level.

See Fig. 13.41E for the finished setting job. Each corner appears
to have four beads, although only one holds the stone. The large
center bead is a protective bead, the two side beads merely ornamental, while the other bead is doing the job of securing the stone.
Since the illusion-type mounting is fashioned so that all beads are
raised, very little trim-up work is necessary. All that is required is
to clean out any metal burrs remaining between the beads and to
bring all beads to a high polish.

While an illusion-type setting is generally adaptable to a fairly wide range of sizes, the stone must be matched very closely to the correct mounting. There is no leeway for squeezing in or spreading outward to accommodate stones that do not really fit the mounting.

Star Mountings

Of all the variations in mounting designs, the comparatively new "star" design appears to be unlike any other. The unique, modern motif of the design is perhaps the most delicate and least bulky in appearance of all the mountings. While it may appear at first glance to be set using an entirely different method, the underlying principle is the same; to push a metal prong over the girdle of the diamond.

See Fig. 13.42A for the side view of the completed setting job and Fig. 13.42B for the top view.

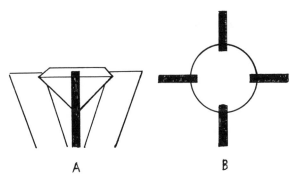

A   B

Fig. 13.42. Completed star setting: *A*, side view; *B*, top view.

At this stage the beginner should understand the method of pushing any prong or bead over a stone. The one problem with the "star" design for the beginner is to understand how to shape the metal that is to serve as a prong. See Fig. 13.43A, which illustrates how a flat graver may be shaped and used in much the same manner as the round graver was used when forming beads (see Flat-top Mountings). The face-angle of the graver is blunter, more than 45 per cent, than the graver used in trimming the flat-top.

It is used in preference to the round graver simply because the thin width of the prong surface would cause the round graver to slide off, whereas the wide flat graver provides a safer cutting edge.

The prong is pushed over the diamond in conventional fashion. The excess metal, shown in Fig. 13.43A, is then filed away and the surfaces polished.

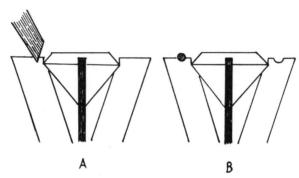

A   B

Fig. 13.43.   Creating a prong or claw: *A,* using the flat graver; *B,* using rat-tail file.

In Fig. 13.43B, a small rat-tail file is used to form the prong instead of the flat graver. The advantage is obvious since the depth of the file cut is easier to control than the depth of a graver cut. The pusher will complete the work and excess metal is filed away.

Great care should be taken to preserve the sharp edges of the "Star" prongs and to see that all prongs are level with each other and parallel with the table of the stone. Due to the severe design, the slightest deviation from the parallel condition is easily noted. Therefore, the new problem in setting a stone in the "Star" mounting is coping with five parallel surfaces—the table of the stone and the four prong surfaces.

Tube Settings

1. In a proper selection of tube settings, it is possible to select one that fits the stone without burring the seat. If the exact tube cannot be found, select one that is slightly larger in diameter than the stone.

2. Select a drill of the same diameter as the tube and drill through the ring (Fig. 13.44A, B).

3. Place the tube in position and solder (Fig. 13.44C).

4. Pickle the ring and dry.

5. Select and sink a burr measuring the same in diameter as the

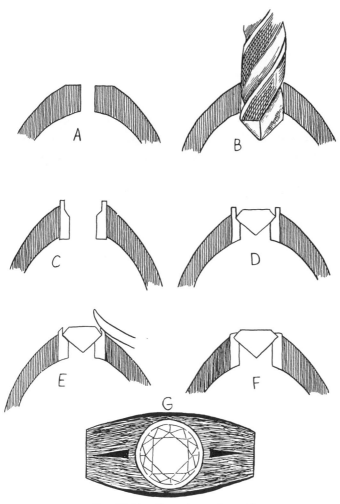

Fig. 13.44.   Steps in a tube setting.

stone (Fig. 13.44D)—that is, if the tube selected does not fit exactly.

6. Place the stone in the setting. With a curved burnisher (Fig. 13.45), burnish the excess metal over the edge of the stone (Fig. 13.44E). Very little metal is needed to secure the stone. A large thick lip of metal will hide and reduce the visible size of the stone.

FIG. 13.45.   Curved burnisher.

To burnish, rub back and forth. The burnisher should be highly polished. If too much metal is seen to appear above the edge of the stone, it may be filed away before burnishing over. If too much metal is burnished over the edges of the stone the excess may be trimmed away with a highly polished flat graver. Fig. 13.44F shows the finished job. Fig. 13.44G shows the top view.

7. Buff lightly.

8. Wash in the cleaning solution.

9. Dip in alcohol and dry in sawdust.

Bezel Settings

1. To make a bezel, wrap binding wire around the girdle of the stone (Fig. 13.46A) and twist as shown in Fig. 13.46B.

2. Remove and cut (Fig. 13.46C). Straighten the wire.

3. Saw a piece of thin stock to the exact length of the wire. The stock may be rolled to the desired thinness.

4. Select a narrower strip of metal and solder the two strips together in the manner shown in Fig. 13.46D and E.

5. Shape the soldered strip as shown in Fig. 13.46F and G.

6. Solder this joint using solder matching the gold in karat.

7. Using a half-round file, shape the bottom of the bezel to fit the contour of the ring (Fig. 13.46H and I). The bezel may be placed over the correct size on the ring mandrel in checking the fit (Fig. 13.46J).

8. Place the bezel in position over the ring and solder, using low-karat solder (Fig. 13.46L). Pickle.

9. Place the stone in the bezel seat and check to see that it is resting level. If not, trim with a flat graver until stone is level (Fig. 13.46M).

10. With a burnisher gradually burnish over the metal by rubbing back and forth all around (Fig. 13.46N). Carefully burnish so that edges do not ripple (see Fig. 13.47 for method).

11. Excess metal may be filed away or bright-cut with a flat tool,

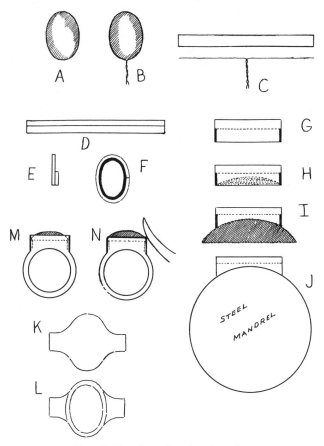

FIG. 13.46. Steps in a bezel setting.

depending on the texture of the stone. The bezel over a soft stone must be bright-cut, for soft stones will not stand direct polishing. The bezel over a hard stone may be finely filed and polished at the machine.

12. Polish the entire ring. Wash and dry in sawdust.

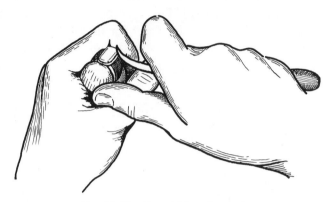

FIG. 13.47.   Burnishing the setting.

Many bezel-type settings, particularly those designed for men's rings, do not use a hand-burnishing technique of securing the stone. To tighten stones set in this type of bezel, the steel punches illustrated in Fig. 12.6 are used to good advantage.

The tightening method is hardly a problem since a punch is selected to fit the ledge (see Fig. 13.48). By placing the ring on a steel mandrel and placing one end of the mandrel in a hole in the bench, both hands are free, one to hold the punch and the other to hold the hammer during the tapping operation.

During the process of tapping, the punch (always held flat) should be moved back and forth to avoid making nicks and to preserve a smooth surface. Tightening a bezel-type mounting where the metal completely surrounds the edge of the stone is a very precarious operation in some cases. Small, smoothly polished burnishers should be used, since they will curl the metal over evenly and leave a smooth finish without ripples or nicks.

The burnisher is a very dangerous tool to use close to the stone, for the slightest touch or pressure on the stone may mar or spoil it, depending on its hardness and durability. Many stones, such as cameos and intaglios, are of very soft substance and will not withstand the slightest scrape.

FIG. 13.48.   Using a punch.

The ring is best held in the ring clamp for burnisher tightening. A selection of curved and straight burnishers should be at hand for tightening this type of bezel. A very safe way to approach the operation is to carefully brace the ring clamp against the bench pin in the manner shown in Fig. 1.5.

A situation that arises all too frequently is the stone that continues to become loose. This is an annoyance to the customer as well as to the repairman and is sometimes the fault of neither. It happens because there was never enough metal forming the bezel to hold the stone securely from the beginning.

Variations

After the novice stonesetter has mastered the seven styles presented above, he will encounter numerous variations in actual practice when mountings from stock are given him for setting. Many of these mountings may appear to be different from anything discussed in this text so far. Hence, a separate study of these variations is in order. Moreover, some heads may be treated in more than one way—either beaded or clawed.

The common head shown in Fig. 13.49 is a variation of the flat-

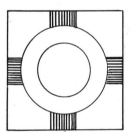

Fig. 13.49.   Flat-top variation.

top. For the sake of clarity we shall show the top view only, as it develops from a blank to the finished product.

Depending on the size of the stone and the area of the top surface, the setting job may develop into a one-bead, two-bead, three-bead, or even four-bead job. If there is little metal area left after the seat is burred, only one bead could be used for maximum security. A little more area would indicate the use of two beads in one corner, both engaging the stone. If a greater metal area is left after burring, then three or four beads may be used. In a three-bead situation, two would grip the stone and one would be idle. In the sequence we are following here, three beads are idle and serve only to embellish the setting.

We begin by shaping the center bead, as in Fig. 13.50. The two long cuts to the girdle position are made with a knife-edge graver; cuts *A–B* and *A–C* are both made from *A*. The cut *D–E* is made

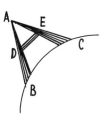

FIG. 13.50. Shaping the beads—preliminary cuts.

by placing a round graver in a position halfway between *B–C* and point *A*. It is not actually a cut, but rather a digging in for depth in order to form an island of metal. (We are primarily concerned here with visualizing the bead or beads as they take shape.)

In Fig. 13.51, we see two islands of metal at *A* and *B*. *A* will become an idle bead, while *B* is taking shape as the primary duty-bead. It is now beginning to bend over the stone through the use of the beading tool.

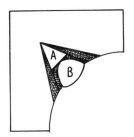

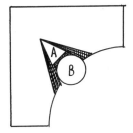

FIG. 13.51. Securing the duty-bead against the stone.

FIG. 13.52. Final shaping of the duty-bead.

In Fig. 13.52, the duty-bead *B* is complete. It is in position against the stone and the setting of the stone is done. The remaining work is trimming and ornamentation.

Fig. 13.53 shows how four different islands of metal have been formed with gravers and shaped using beading tools. The "carving" using gravers is executed in much the same manner as explained in Fig. 13.50. The cuts begin at *E* and *D*. When the islands are formed the beading tools are used to create the rounded bead.

Fig. 13.54 shows the final product. Here we see that all excess metal has been trimmed away (using flat gravers) leaving four beads in relief.

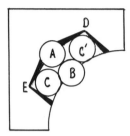

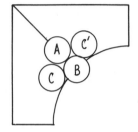

FIG. 13.53. Forming side beads at *C* and *C'*.

FIG. 13.54. The completed operations.

In Fig. 13.55 we see a similar head; however, the space between the corners is deeper, suggesting a claw-type setting rather than the flat-top method (the flat-top is permissible; the decision is up to the setter).

In Fig. 13.56 two saw cuts are made at *A–B* and *C–D*. The

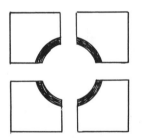

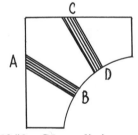

FIG. 13.55. Flat-top variation.

FIG. 13.56. Cuts preliminary to forming claws.

depth of the cuts is to the depth of the girdle position. Do not use a saw blade that may remove too much metal (too thick), for the remaining metal may not be enough to hold the stone securely. By the same token, do not use a saw blade that is too thin, for later you will have to devote extra time to trimming-out between the three islands of metal.

In Fig. 13.57 claw-shaping is in progress. Using a jeweler's bar-

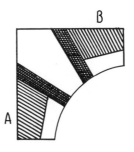

Fig. 13.57. Forming claws with the jeweler's barrette file.

rette file with smoothed edges the claw tips are weakened at the areas *A* and *B*. The claws or prongs are gradually weakened until they may be bent over the edge of the stone. Too much effort in coaxing the tips to bend is an indication of too heavy a prong. File away until the claw bends more readily, yet is heavy enough to provide safety for years of wear.

In Fig. 13.58 the claws appear to be stretching over the stone.

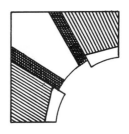

Fig. 13.58. Appearance of claws as they are bent over girdle.

From a side view, it would be evident that the claw is not stretching but merely bending over the edge of the stone. In Fig. 13.59 the final bending has been accomplished. The eight claws are snugly over the stone. The next operation is "cleaning-up" or finishing the work.

Fig. 13.60 illustrates two types of finished claws (obviously not used on the same setting job). It is the setter's prerogative to use either the square method (*A*) or the pointed method (*B*). Note that the island (*C*) has been rounded and shaped as have the outer edges of claws *A* and *B*. To remove burrs from the sawed cuts, a small flat tool may be used. By small we mean a #36 or smaller. Smaller ones are made by flattening the belly of a knife-edge graver thus enabling it to execute a polished flat cut tapering upward.

In finishing up this type of head, polished gravers may be used for all trim work to eliminate the necessity for exposing the surfaces to the polishing lathe. For example, beginning at *D* and trimming to *E* with a highly polished flat graver, a sharp-faceted appearance may be attained, which is frequently lost as it is presented to the polishing lathe.

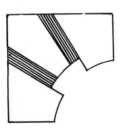

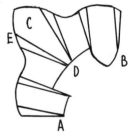

Fig. 13.59. Bending is completed: claws snug over girdle.

Fig. 13.60. The finished claws: *A*, the square claw; *B*, the pointed claw.

The student must expect different shapes in flat-top mountings and must learn to improvise or adapt the method of trimming to suit the job. See Fig. 13.12 for examples. Fig. 13.12F shows a variation of the flat-top mounting. Fig. 13.12G shows a square flat-top setting with a double row of milgraining. The extra row is formed with the knife-edge tool, cutting a groove behind the first row of milgraining and thus forming a second edge.

An advantage in using two or even more rows of milgraining arises when setting a stone that is too small for the size of the mounting selected. It becomes necessary to fill the extra space with milgraining, a course preferable to trimming out completely from the edge of the stone.

Fig. 13.12H–L shows the successive steps in setting a stone in another variation of a flat-top setting, one that is adaptable to many mountings of both ladies' and men's rings. This particular style, while highly acceptable in appearance, has one outstanding characteristic not on the credit side. Owing to the nature of the design, it has more than its share of sharp corners and seems to have a particular affinity for catching or snagging clothing, especially ladies' hose.

In setting a stone in this type of mounting it is advisable to double-check carefully all corners for sharp edges or burrs. One good method is to rub the finished setting job over cloth that has a deep nap. The burrs or sharp edges are sure to catch and pull away short lengths of fiber. On examination with a loupe the troublesome areas are located by the bits of hair or fiber wedged beneath burrs or sharp edges.

In Fig. 13.61 we see a diamond placed over the head of a modern, simple four-prong mounting. Fig. 13.62 is the side view of the

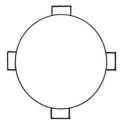

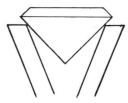

Fig. 13.61. Direct view of stone in position over prongs.

Fig. 13.62. Side view of stone resting on prongs.

head before setting proceeds. Fig. 13.63 shows two prongs and girdle, one prong being pushed and one prong before the pushing treatment. The prong tips may be left square as shown or they may be pointed as seen in Fig. 13.64.

In Fig. 13.65 we see a deviation from the conventional. This is an attractive head, the square appearance of which displays the stone to good advantage, using a square-shaped prong. See Fig. 13.66.

Fig. 13.67 is another variation of the modern treatment where the bead is partially formed. Fig. 13.68 shows the completed job. It is well to observe the advantages of the particular head. It is

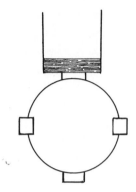

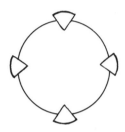

FIG. 13.63.   Prong tips being pushed over girdle of stone.

FIG. 13.64.   Completed setting.

adaptable to a wide range of sizes, but many other designs are restricted to diamonds of a given diameter.

See Fig. 13.69 for a view of a more modern fishtail mounting before setting. The completed job, Fig. 13.70, clearly shows how

FIG. 13.65.   Head before setting the stone.

FIG. 13.66.   Head after setting the stone.

the two corner prongs are shaped to hold the stone securely and neatly.

Fig. 13.71 may not be conventional in appearance, but the setting technique presents no new method. It is the same bead method used in the conventional flat-top but so designed that the setter is concerned with the head only. All the laborious trim work is eliminated. See Fig. 13.72 for the appearance after setting.

Fig. 13.67. The head before setting procedures.

Fig. 13.68. Its appearance after the stone is set.

Fig. 13.69. The head before setting procedures, a fishtail mounting.

Fig. 13.70. Appearance after setting the stone.

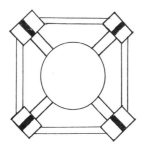

Fig. 13.71. The head prior to setting the stone.

Fig. 13.72. The head after setting the stone.

Setting Variations of Standard Heads

Fig. 13.73 shows a top-view of a standard four-prong head. This is a very simple setting job, and after seating the stone the prongs may be pushed over and shaped as seen in Fig. 13.74.

FIG. 13.73.   View of four-prong head before setting procedures.

FIG. 13.74.   View of head after stone is set.

Fig. 13.75 is a very attractive variation that is highly acceptable. This effect is made by splitting each prong using a jeweler's saw. The result is eight prongs instead of four.

Fig. 13.76 shows a broad prong slightly tapered on the sides. The tip of the prong may be beveled by using a #38 flat graver, highly polished.

Fig. 13.77 shows the split-prong variation with each prong tapered.

FIG. 13.75.   The split-prong variation.

FIG. 13.76.   A broad, tapered-prong variation.

Fig. 13.78 shows a differently shaped, single-prong treatment. A rounded taper is given each prong.

It is well to acquire the knack of instantly deciding just which treatment should be given to the setting job. The design of the mounting and the method used on the smaller side-diamonds (if any) are the guiding factors.

Fig. 13.79 shows the top view of a very common mounting.

Fig. 13.80 illustrates one method of treating the prongs which is very similar to the fishtail treatment.

FIG. 13.77.   The tapered, split-prong variation.

FIG. 13.78.   The tapered, single-prong variation.

Fig. 13.81 shows a very pleasing and flattering method of setting the same stone in the same head. The edges are milgrained.

Fig. 13.82 shows the top of a flat-top setting before beginning the setting job. There is plenty of metal to work with and this head will accommodate a wide range of sizes. If the stone is large,

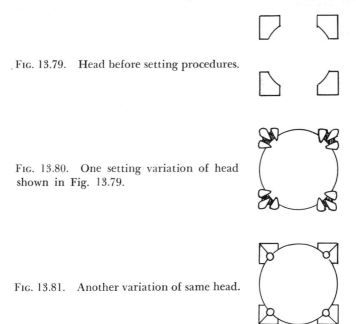

FIG. 13.79.   Head before setting procedures.

FIG. 13.80.   One setting variation of head shown in Fig. 13.79.

FIG. 13.81.   Another variation of same head.

the treatment seen in Fig. 13.83 is indicated. If the stone is small, the method as shown in Fig. 13.84 will flatter the stone. By using three rows of milgraining, all of the area is utilized. To use the method shown in Fig. 13.83 would be to direct attention to a small stone in a large head. The three rows of milgraining minimize that effect.

Fig. 13.82.   Flat-top before setting procedures.

Fig. 13.83.   Conventional setting treatment for flat-top.

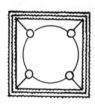

Fig. 13.84.   Triple row of milgraining to make small stone appear larger.

Setting Small Stones

Let us examine Fig. 13.85 which shows a lady's wedding band, set with five small diamonds. This style of setting is the simple

Fig. 13.85.   The final appearance.

flat-top style used frequently for mounting men's large solitaires. Mounting the five stones requires a knack of close estimation, for the stones have to be spaced, if not equally, then at least in a manner pleasing to the eye. It is not always possible to space stones equally because the diameters at the girdle are almost never exactly the same. It would be most wise to place the largest stone in the center, the next larger two beside it, and the two smaller stones on the ends.

The mounting usually comes to the jeweler looking like Fig. 13.86. It is up to him to measure carefully the five stones and de-

FIG. 13.86. The mounting before work is begun.

cide then and there if they will work in the given mounting.

Assuming that they will work, cautiously proceed to burr out the openings designated for each stone. (This is done by selecting a burr slightly smaller in diameter than the stone to be mounted —the burrs make openings slightly larger than their diameters.) Using the flexible shaft machine, this operation is completed in seconds. Rather than complete the mounting of one stone at a time, it is better to anchor all five in their respective positions. This will allow for freedom in "trimming up" and "finishing off" the setting job.

This anchoring is done by "working up" four beads to hold each stone. Each bead is in a square or corner position. See Fig. 13.87E.

Fig. 13.87 illustrates the progressive steps of setting a small dia-

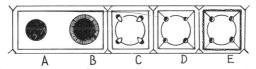

FIG. 13.87. Consecutive steps in setting the stones.

mond or melee from the burring out of the seat (A) through the final trimming up (E).

In setting small stones, it is not usually necessary to weaken the sides of the bead before pushing it over the stone, since it may be easily pushed over with a small round-belly graver #50 or #51.

To "work up" this bead, simply place the graver in position and wiggle it from side to side as the rear section or handle is gradually lifted upward. This movement "throws" a small burr (later it is a bead) against the stone. Needless to say, the procedure is to anchor opposite corners respectively in order to obtain a level table. One word of caution—a bead is not made by digging into the metal with pressure forward, toward the girdle of the stone. Contrary to the beginner's idea, the pressure at the tip is downward and away from the girdle. Then there is little danger of slipping forward and cutting off the bead completely. The shape of the face of the graver (if about 55°) will be a wedge that forces the bead forward as the tip works itself deeper. It is not the particular effort of the stonesetter that gets the bead over the girdle; it is the wedge-shaped graver that does the work as it bites deeper into the metal.

When each stone is snug in its seat, each burr may be slightly rounded into a bead by using one of the beading tools. This will establish a uniform size for all the beads and will isolate bits of metal that will be trimmed away later.

At this stage, study the distance between each stone to determine whether there is need for a double or single row of milgraining. If the area seems to call for a double or single row of milgraining, then, using a knife-edge graver, make a single cut midway between each stone. See Fig. 13.87. Later, when the individual settings are trimmed, this groove will help furnish a knife-edge ridge over which the final milgrain tool will travel.

Select a flat graver of a width suitable to small settings. A #36 or #38 will do very well. Trim away all excess metal around the girdle of each stone, remembering that a highly polished graver leaves a highly polished surface. Be especially careful while cutting close to the sharp edges needed for the milgrain tool—these must be carefully preserved.

Before using the milgrain tool for the final step, carefully check the firmness of each stone and the roundness of each bead. If they need touching up, now is the time to do it.

Very carefully milgrain all prepared edges and the job is complete.

The stones just discussed, set in individual flat-top settings, might very easily (and more quickly) have been set in a modern channel mounting. Usually stones to be set in channel mountings are of a nearly equal diameter since the finished job must be neat and regular, and without the bulge that an outsize stone would make. See Fig. 13.88.

Fig. 13.88.   Melee in channel mounting.

This type of mounting is particularly adaptable to the setting of many very small diamonds. (Sometimes diamonds are set in this manner, running completely around the band, with no break or plain gold band showing—or platinum, as the case may be.) These are placed in a channel, girdles resting on a race or ledge already prepared for such stones. They are placed side by side, girdles barely touching. The two top edges of the channel are burnished over the stones in long sweeping strokes with a highly polished steel burnisher. While some edges may be left plain, depending on the design of the mounting, most of this style are milgrained to further insure the tightness of the stones and to add to the beauty of the design.

Some channel mountings may have single holes drilled for a specific number of stones. In this case the stones must be of very exact measurement. To insure their stability, slight seats are burred out and the only other concern is to see that all remain level as the channel edge is burnished or milgrained over the girdle of each stone. Here, again, dimensions must be fairly exact for, to insure the desired beauty of setting, the girdles of each stone must be side by side.

Removing Stones from Mountings

Stones from old or worn-out mountings may be removed by the method that is considered to be the safest. Each type of mounting may indicate a different method of removal. For example, stones in flat-top mountings may easily be removed by cutting away the beads gripping the stone (using a flat graver). If the stone does not lift out using tapered beeswax, it may be lightly pushed from underneath using pegwood. Of course, too much resistance indicates something is still gripping the stone and it should be re-examined to see that no tiny burr of metal is over the girdle edge. When the girdle is free the stone will adhere to the beeswax.

Tiffany prong tips may be filed away if they are heavy or lifted up using the wedge shape of a flat graver if they are thin or pliable. The latter method may be dangerous to the very soft stones but not at all to the diamond, remembering that it is suggested only if the prong tips are worn and weak. A heavy prong must be cut or filed away. Fishtail prongs may be removed in the same manner.

In removing any valuable stone, mutilating the old mounting is of little consideration as compared with mutilating the stone during removal. With practice, the stones may be removed with a minimum of cutting or filing of the old mountings, which are frequently returned to the customer.

Chapter 14

Repairing Mountings

Repairing prongs—flame method
Repairing prongs—electric-machine method
Replacing worn mounting tops
Installing new heads

Repairing Prongs—Flame Method

Repairing prongs takes us into several different categories or styles of mountings—the Tiffany, the basket setting, the fishtail, and even the flat-top mounting that is minus a bead or beads. Methods of repairing these prongs depend a great deal on how large the stone is and also on the nature of the metal. Ordinary yellow- or white-gold prongs may be soldered in position without removing the diamond or ruby provided it is a real or synthetic ruby; imitation rubies will not stand the heat.

Following is the step-by-step procedure for repairing prongs on a Tiffany mounting:

1. Clean the broken tip thoroughly (Fig. 14.1A).
2. Apply flux and lay a small square of solder over the tip of the prong.
3. Holding the shank of the ring in the bench vise, use a small blue flame to flow the solder over the tip.
4. Holding a small strip of gold in soldering tweezers (prong wire may be used) place in position over the broken prong. Apply

flame again and solder. Do not forget to flux the gold piece (Fig. 14.1B).

5. File away excess metal as shown in Fig. 14.1D. Shape to match other prongs.

6. With a prong pusher, lay over the prong flush with the stones (Fig. 14.1E).

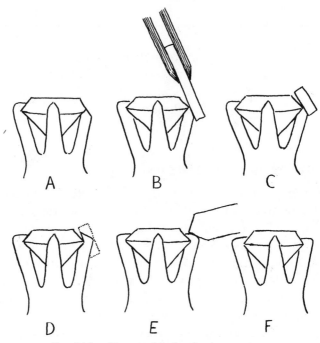

Fig. 14.1.   Flame-soldering broken prongs.

7. Pickle the ring and buff, being careful to refinish all prongs alike so that the repaired prong cannot be detected.

8. Wash and dry. Fig. 14.1F shows the completed job.

Warning! Only a diamond, ruby, reconstructed ruby, or stone of equal hardness will stand soldering in this manner. On soft stones it is necessary to lift up the tips of the prongs, remove the stone, replace the broken prong, and reset the stone.

If the prong is broken off nearer the base, it is usually necessary to remove the stone by prying up all the prong tips, using a flat graver as a wedge, carefully and gently wiggling from side to side (see Fig. 14.2). A piece of gold slightly longer and slightly wider than the original prong is soldered in position after filing the ends as shown in Fig. 14.3. This method of filing gives a larger grasping surface, a larger and more secure joint. After soldering, the prong

Fig. 14.2. Using the graver.

Fig. 14.3. Fitting for the new prong.

Fig. 14.4. Using the pliers.

is filed to shape. It is now in a straight position in contrast to the other prongs, which have seat indentations and are bent in position. The girdle seat may be provided on this one prong by using a jeweler's file of a rounded shape. The bend forward toward the stone may be accomplished by using ordinary snipe-nose pliers (see Fig. 14.4) to give it a start. The stone may be placed in position and all prongs tightened securely, using the prong pusher.

During the process of working with all prongs, burrs or rough edges may occur. Each prong must be closely examined. Any suspicious sharp edge should be rounded slightly and burrs removed.

Repairing Prongs—Electric-Machine Method

1. Clean the prong thoroughly (Fig. 14.5A).
2. Apply flux, place a small square of solder over the tip of the prong, and flow the solder, using a well-shaped carbon pencil (Fig. 14.5B).

3. Holding the prong wire as shown in Fig. 14.5C, place the carbon pencil in contact and solder.

4. Reshape and finish the prong in the manner explained above under Repairing Prongs—Flame Method.

The same procedures for repairing prongs or claws may be followed on all other styles of mountings except, of course, the flat-top styles.

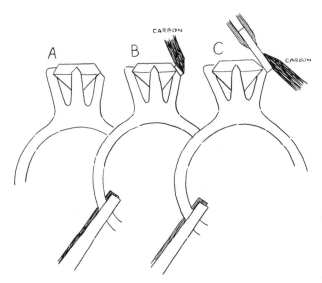

FIG. 14.5.   Machine-soldering broken prongs.

Replacing Worn Mounting Tops

1. Fig. 14.6A shows a badly worn top that will eventually wear through and cause the stone to drop out. If the ring is worn as badly in other places, it would be advisable to set the diamond or stone in a new mounting. However, a new top may be soldered on and the ring restored as good as new. To do this, remove the stone by cutting away the remaining metal or prongs. This may be done with a #40 flat tool. Sometimes the tips may be lifted away from the stone by carefully using the flat tool as a wedge. Do not risk

chipping the stone by using too much force. If the tips are stubborn, it is far better to cut them away and remove the stone with
beeswax. This method is foolproof and there is little danger of

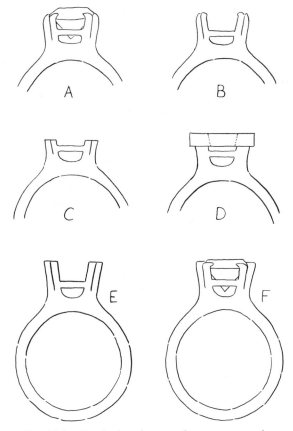

Fig. 14.6.   Replacing the top of a worn mounting.

cracking the edges of the stone. Fig. 14.6B shows the prongs after
the removal of the stone.

2. File away the worn top (Fig. 14.6C).

3. Shape a square of stock to the approximate size of the filed
ring top (Fig. 14.6D).

4. Place the square piece in position and solder. Remember to

prepare the surfaces and flux properly. One simple method of applying the solder is to flux the four corners of the top or head, apply a square of solder over each corner, and using the flame, flow the solder. Flux the square of stock, place in position over the ring top and heat until the solder flows at all four corners. As this happens, the square of stock will settle absolutely flush, and the new top is secure (Fig. 14.6D).

5. Carefully file and shape the new top to the shape and size of the old head.

6. With the jeweler's saw, saw out the four slots in the sides as shown by dotted lines in Fig. 14.6D. Finish the edge with a fine file.

7. The head is now ready for resetting the stone (Fig. 14.6E). The procedures are the same as explained in Chapter 13 under Fish-tail Mountings. Fig. 14.6F shows the finished job.

The above method of repairing a head may seem to be the long way around since one could replace the entire head. However, the method is worth knowing and will come in handy if a new head is not immediately available.

It is possible to secure complete heads from houses specializing in jewelers' findings and materials. Should a new head be required, it is necessary to select carefully the right size for the stone.

Installing New Heads

To replace a worn head, first create outward tension in the ring shank by placing it on the steel mandrel. Tap it gently downward in the manner shown in Fig. 14.7. Then, using a torch and holding the ring in the position shown in Fig. 14.8, heat the head until the solder melts between head and shank. Usually the tension created will cause the joints to spring open and allow the head to fall out. If it does not fall out, a little "coaxing" with any long tapered piece of metal will do the trick.

To prepare the shank for the new head, clean the entire shank thoroughly using the pickle solution, then file the joints flush (see Fig. 14.9). Insert the head in position to test the angle of filing (Fig. 14.10). Since the shank was opened slightly during the first operation, a slight closing bend using ring bending pliers will bring the joints into proper alignment (Fig. 14.11).

Since no excess solder is wanted (that might run over the shank or head), it is advisable to flow small amounts of solder on the

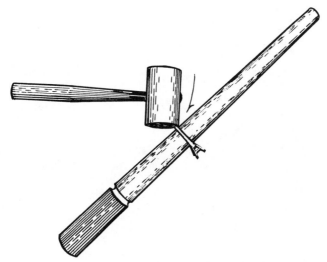

Fig. 14.7. Adding tension to shank.

shank (see Fig. 14.12). Then "rough up" the surface on the head at exactly the point of contact between shank and head. Carefully apply the flux to this area only. Clamp the shank to the asbestos soldering block as shown in Fig. 14.13. Place the head in position and solder both joints at once.

When more experience in soldering has been acquired, the op-

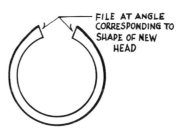

Fig. 14.8. Position for removing a head.

Fig. 14.9. Preparation of shank for new head.

eration may be accomplished from the position shown in Fig. 14.14. Of course, the head must rest in place without any tension from the shank, for, during the heating, the expansion of metal would cause it to rise out of position.

FIG. 14.10.   Fitting the head.

FIG. 14.11.   Head in correct position.

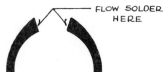

FIG. 14.12.   Preparation of shank for soldering.

New heads for differently shaped mountings may be replaced in a manner similar to that described above. On a flat-top mounting, the old top may be filed away or removed by melting the old solder joint. Replacements are available from suppliers in a variety of shapes.

For worn bezel-type mountings, complete new bezels for standard size stones may be purchased, soldered on, and the stone reset.

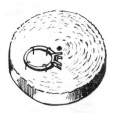

FIG. 14.13.   Clamping shank with head to asbestos soldering pad.

FIG. 14.14.   Holding shank with the head upright.

Chapter 15

Plating

THE JEWELER has become more and more aware of the necessity for providing repair customers with faster and more complete professional services. The delay in sending repair and plating jobs to trade houses is an unavoidable hazard to customer relationship and, following the trend to do more work on the premises, plating has been added as a valuable feature.

The advantages are manifold. For conventional repair jobs such as ring sizing and miscellaneous soldering, flash plating as a final operation will enhance the article so greatly that the customers are frequently stunned at the "like new" appearance. Obviously, turning out such perfectly finished work builds prestige and additional business.

Another advantage is the ability to do rhodium plating on the premises, an operation that has become increasingly so important that it probably overshadows the value of all the other plating mediums, particularly for stores enjoying a substantial diamond business.

215

The information and directions and the illustrations in this chapter have been supplied by Hoover & Strong, Inc., Buffalo, New York, and they are used here with their kind permission.*

Building a Plating Bench

As a matter of convenience, it is worthwhile to build a plating bench. A hot plate is needed, either electric or gas, as some solutions must be heated. If gas is used, a metal screen or plate should be used to protect the beakers from direct flame. Two copper bus bars are suspended over the hot plate about 2 inches apart. They are simply rigid copper bars. The bars may be mounted on supports made of wood, transite, or any insulating material. If mounted on metal wall brackets, they should be insulated from

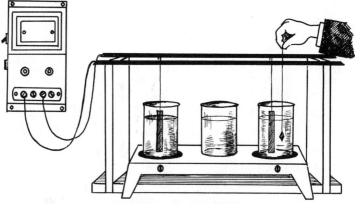

FIG. 15.1.   Plating bench.

the brackets. One bar may be permanently connected to the negative terminal of the plater. It is best to attach a battery clip to the other connecting wire so the connection may be readily shifted to either the 2 volt, 6 volt, or 8 volt terminal. With this arrangement, the anodes are left attached to the positive bus bar, and the wire holding the work to be plated is simply held in contact with the negative bus bar when electro cleaning and plating (see Fig. 15.1).

* Bulletin 347, "Plating Made Easy," © Hoover & Strong, Inc., 1947.

Plating Various Metals

The principle of all types of electroplating is the same. In order to give step-by-step instructions, let us plate a brass cross to a bright yellow finish.

Gold

First, we must prepare the solutions and electrical connections. The Electro Cleaner is diluted as directed on the bottle label and poured into an 800 cc Pyrex beaker to within about an inch of the top. A second beaker is filled with distilled water for rinsing. The third beaker is filled with pure gold plating solution, used full strength.

Connect the stainless steel anode to the 6 volt terminal of the Electro Plater with a copper wire (doorbell wire will do) and then immerse the anode in the cleaner solution, keeping it to one side of the beaker. In the same way connect a pure gold * anode also to the 6 volt terminal and immerse it in the pure gold solution.

The Electro Cleaner and pure gold solutions are heated to 180° F, and we are ready to proceed.

The cross is first polished with jewelers' rouge to produce the desired high luster. Then, it is fastened to a copper wire and cleaned by boiling in a solution of soap and water with a little baking soda and ammonia added. Use a brush if necessary.

Do not expect to get an adherent deposit or uniform plating unless the article is clean. From this point on it should not be touched with the fingers.

The free end of the wire holding the cross is connected to the negative terminal of the plater, and the switch is turned on. The cross is removed from the soap solution, rinsed in water, and plated in the following steps.

1. Immerse the cross in the Electro Cleaner solution for about 30 seconds, jiggling it at the end of the wire.

* If you do not have a gold anode, you may use a stainless steel anode for a few jobs as explained later under Life of Solutions.

2. Rinse in water.

3. Immerse in the pure gold plating solution for 30 to 60 seconds, again jiggling the cross at the end of the wire. Rinse in water and the job is done. (See Fig. 15.2.)

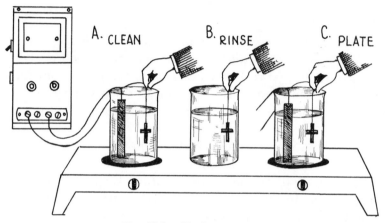

FIG. 15.2.   Plating a cross.

All flash plating is done in the same way. However, each kind of plating solution has its own requirements of temperature, voltage, and kind of anode; each type of finish calls for a certain technique in polishing; and certain metals such as stainless steel require special preparation. In the ensuing pages we will try to clarify each type of procedure. There is nothing complicated to do, but a full understanding is the easiest means to success.

Silver

Silver has tremendous throwing power and will accordingly come out of the solution a little milky or dull. It will therefore be necessary to run over it again with the scratch brush and buff.

Since one Electro Plater will handle up to 238 square inches of surface, and the solution does not have to be heated, you might wish to set up a larger tank. Use a 2- or 5-gallon stoneware jar and arrange several silver anodes around the tank as shown in the set-up for plating baby shoes (Fig. 15.4), connecting the anodes to the 2 volt terminal. The wires may be permanently connected to the plater as no current will pass except when it is in use.

In plating a deep hollow object like a water pitcher, it may be necessary to lower one of the anodes into the pitcher.

It is sometimes desired to gold plate the inside of silver articles, for example, a sugar bowl. This can be done by filling the bowl with gold solution and dangling the gold anode inside, attaching the negative wire to the handle. If you are not able to fill the bowl quite to the top, get a very small sponge which is soaked in the gold solution, wrap it around the gold anode, and swab this over the surface to be plated. This is, in effect, substantially the same as the so-called brush-plating operation.

Special finishes for silver including "oxidized" and French Gray will be described under "Finishes."

Copper and Nickel

These metals are handled the same as gold, except for their individual requirements of concentration, temperature, voltage, and anodes, as indicated on each bottle label, and no further instructions are required.

Rhodium

Rhodium is a very brilliant, hard, white finish and is not readily attacked by any known substance except at an elevated temperature. Once you get it on, you won't be able to get it off, so make sure you get it on right.

First, the article should be polished to a very high luster and thoroughly cleaned. Spotty cleaning will result in a spotty finish. If a high polish cannot otherwise be obtained, plate the article first with nickel, which will take the desired high polish.

The article is flash plated as gold is, and since rhodium is so hard that it cannot be readily polished, no attempt should be made to build up a heavy deposit. In the event of failure, we suggest plating again with nickel, and repeating the procedure.

Chromium Plating

We do not recommend this operation except in the hands of the experienced plater who can devote full time to the work and has the necessary equipment and controls.

The solution will burn the fingers; the fumes will irritate the nasal membranes, and this can result in permanent injury. The best way to avoid injury is to wear rubber gloves and a respirator mask, as the violent reaction throws up a spray.

The current density must be regulated to exactly 1 amp per square inch of plating surface, and a rheostat and ammeter are required to do this. The temperature must be maintained between 110° and 115° F and the solution will tend to heat up because of its resistance to the current.

Following is the standard formula for chromium plating solution:

Chromic acid	33 ounces
Sulfuric acid	½ fluid dram
Distilled water	1 gallon

Anodes are 6 per cent antimonial lead, preferably ribbed, which should be hung around the tank in various positions so as to surround the work. The total anode surface facing the work should not exceed the total surface of the work.

The slinging wire should be at least as heavy as the article and preferably should be soldered to it. Otherwise it must be firmly attached under tension as with spring clips. No parts may be loose, and articles such as hinged compacts must be fastened under tension so that no motion can take place between the parts.

Commercial platers usually nickel plate and polish the work before plating with chromium, as chromium is difficult to polish because of its hardness.

Hoover & Strong does not furnish supplies for chromium plating. The necessary materials can be obtained from any plating supply dealer.

Finishes

The scratch brush is used wet, and a little glue should be added to the water for lubrication. For special soft effects, powdered pumice may be used with it. The grinding wheel is charged by applying glue to the surface while the wheel is in motion; when nearly dry, 300-grain emery or carborundum powder is applied. A flat piece of wood held against the surface will help work this in, and the wheel will be ready for use when thoroughly dry. Plater supply houses carry prepared compounds containing abrasive grain.

Bear in mind that the texture, the compound, and speed of these wheels do the work; it would be a mistake to apply more pressure than needed to hold the work firmly against the wheels.

The foregoing applies to the preparation of flat and convex outside surfaces. It will be apparent to the reader that end brushes, end wheels, hand brushes, and the like will be necessary to reach inner contours.

English, Butler, and Roman

These finishes depend entirely on the preparation. The color depends on the plating solution. If you want an "English" finish, you will polish the work to the highest possible luster with rouge, and color it by plating in the pure gold solution. If you want a "Butler" finish, you will mat down the surface with the scratch brush, and then color it by plating with gold or silver. The "Roman" finish is a little softer, and is obtained by using pumice powder with the scratch brush. Any of these finishes can just as well be colored white, red, pink, or green, depending on the solution used.

Antique Yellow and Dark Green

For many years jewelers have used "Rose Gold" to describe a reddish-yellow finish applied to an article having a design in deep relief or in separate parts. The highlight is bright and the background is dull. Hoover & Strong formerly sold a solution for this purpose under the name of "Rose Gold." In recent years, the appearance of jewelry made of pink or red golds has led to some confusion, and they have accordingly changed the name of this solution to "Antique Yellow."

Antique Yellow Gold Solution has great throwing power, with the result that the article quickly takes on a frosty, reddish-yellow surface. But when the high spots or "highlights" are rubbed with a little moist baking soda on the tip of the finger, the highlights are brightened and an effect of elegant contrast is produced—like antique jewelry dulled by age, but partially brightened by use.

An antique green finish can be produced in the same way, using Hoover Dark Green Solution. This gives a smutty dark green finish, and is highlighted with baking soda like the antique yellow.

The so-called Oxidized finish is really a sulfide formation generally applied to silver or copper, sometimes to other metals.

Since some scratch brushing and buffing will be required, the plated surface should be given a thick enough deposit to withstand this abrasion.

Make up a solution of 3 ounces Liver of Sulfur to 1 gallon of water. This is used warm for silver, and cold for copper.

The article is polished with rouge, cleaned, and immersed in the solution until uniformly dark. Then it is removed, rinsed, and scratch brushed, and polished in spots to give it the desired mottled or highlighted appearance.

Oxidized articles are generally given a coating of lacquer to prevent the bright areas from tarnishing.

French Gray

This is an oxidized finish applied to silver in the same manner as described above, but it is uniformly scratch brushed or sand blasted to give a uniformly gray color caused by cutting through the dark surface. Such an article should not be lacquered.

Two-toned Finishes

To obtain these finishes, use stop-off lacquer and lacquer thinner. Suppose you have a 10-karat yellow gold signet ring with a white gold Masonic emblem on top. Polish and clean the ring as usual. Apply the stop-off lacquer to the emblem and when the lacquer is dry, plate the ring in the 14-karat gold solution. Then remove the lacquer by soaking in the lacquer thinner. Now coat the gold-plated part with the lacquer, and plate the emblem with rhodium or palladium. Finally remove the lacquer and if necessary run over the ring with the rouge buff.

Another method of applying two or more colors is by means of "brush plating."

Brush Plating

Brush plating is used for local coloring of objects such as the two-toned finishes mentioned above, and for objects which may not conveniently be tank plated.

The simplest type of plating brush for small jewelry work can be made from a medicine dropper as shown in Fig. 15.3.

Fig. 15.3.   Brush plating using medicine dropper.

A small quill brush, in which the bristles are bound with copper wire, is obtained from an artists' supply store and placed in the medicine dropper with the bristles protruding through the discharge aperture. The tube is then filled with the solution to be used, the rubber bulb replaced, and the positive wire is pushed through a hole punctured in the bulb until it comes in contact with the bristles. The positive wire thus serves as the anode. The brush should be adjusted in the discharge aperture so that by squeezing the bulb of the medicine dropper, one drop of solution is discharged. The solution is painted onto the work, one drop at a time, until the desired portions are covered.

An alternative to discharging the solution from the medicine dropper is repeatedly dipping the brush into the solution and painting it onto the article.

Much larger brushes may be used for larger jobs. For example, you can get a 2-inch varnish brush and wrap copper wire around the handle, bringing one end down into the bristles where it will make contact with the solution and complete the circuit. The solution is then painted onto the work as described above.

Since the metal ferrule holding the bristles might act itself as an anode, care must be taken to keep it out of the solution where it would cause contamination. On prolonged jobs, the brush should be rinsed out from time to time.

Another method of making a plating "brush" is to take a piece of glass tubing and insert a small sponge in one end and a cork in the other end, leading the positive wire through a hole in the cork and filling the tube with solution.

Plating Baby Shoes

Remove the lace and clean both the shoe and the lace by scrubbing with soap or cleaning fluid; allow to dry thoroughly.

Apply a coat of white shellac, which may be thinned a little with alcohol so that it will readily enter the pores of the leather. Treat the center two-thirds of the lace with shellac. Allow the shoe and lace to dry in a warm place. Excessive heat may crack the shellac.

Lace up the shoe and tie the ends of the laces, which have not been covered with the first coat of shellac, allowing them to drape naturally. Apply a second coat of shellac to the entire shoe. As the shellac dries it will hold the laces in the desired position. When it becomes tacky, pull up the tongue and the shellac will hold it in place. Allow to dry.

A conductive surface is produced by applying copper bronze powder mixed with lacquer. Mix $\frac{1}{2}$ ounce lacquer thinner and $\frac{1}{2}$ ounce clear lacquer. Stir in 1 ounce (by volume) of very fine copper bronze powder, which can be obtained from a paint store. Make sure that you get copper, not an aluminum-colored powder that resembles copper. The powder must be free from oil, which may be removed with carbon tetrachloride ("Carbona") if present. Apply a coat of this mixture, let dry, and apply a second coat.

The mixture is intended to contain just enough lacquer to make the powder adhere, and the surface should look frosty when dry.

A super glaze indicates excess lacquer which will "stop off" the conductivity and should be corrected in the second coat by adding more thinner. All parts of the shoe, lace, eyelets, and the inside of the top must be coated.

Rinse the shoe in running water before placing in the plating bath. This is to remove any excess copper powder and aids in obtaining a smooth deposit.

For the tank use a 5-gallon stone jar, obtainable from any hardware store. Place in it 5 pounds copper sulfate and 3 gallons distilled water. While stirring vigorously, cautiously add 12 fluid ounces sulfuric acid, and finally add 1½ teaspoons of corn syrup. When the copper sulfate is dissolved, let stand in a cool place for several hours until the temperature of the solution drops to about 60° F. Do not redissolve any crystals that may have precipitated out. Filter and replace in the tank.*

Now run a copper wire around the top of the tank, under the rim, and connect one end to the 6 volt terminal of the Electro Plater. To this wire attach 4 copper anodes as shown in Fig. 15.4. The anodes should be withdrawn from the solution when not in use. Place a stick of wood across the top of the tank, and run a copper wire, the heavier the better, on top of the stick to act as a bus bar. Connect this to the negative terminal.

Make a sling to hold the baby shoe by winding a copper wire twice around a quart fruit jar. Keep an extra 8 inches at the short end and twist the wires together where the two loops are complete.

Spread the two loops out and place the shoe in them and then bend the short end down into the shoe to hold it under tension and keep it from floating out of the sling. The long end of the

---

* This is not the same as prepared Hoover Copper Plating Solution, which contains cyanide. The cyanide solution is better for flash plating; the acid sulfate is better for heavier deposits. Never mix the two kinds together, for lethal hydrocyanic acid gas would be formed.

wire is wound once or twice around the bus bar to make good contact.

Place a few nuts or bolts inside the toe to keep the shoe from floating. The plater should be turned on when the shoe is immersed and it will be necessary to push the shoe down with a stick of wood until it is completely submerged. The solution should be used at 70° F room temperature.

Let the plating operation continue an hour or so, and then

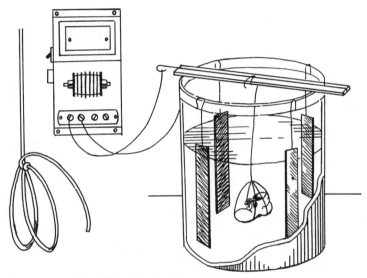

Fig. 15.4.   Method for plating baby shoes.

bring the shoe out for examination, but rinse in running water before handling. It may develop a surface roughness in certain places called "orange peel," which is usually caused by having the shoe too close to one of the anodes, or because the conductive coating is too heavy in spots. Any orange peel is smoothed down with emery cloth, and the shoe is returned to the tank. Four or five hours will give a firm coating, but all night is better.

When it is finally removed from the bath, the shoe is rinsed in running water and any additional orange peel is removed with emery cloth. The whole shoe is then rubbed with steel wool and dipped in moist Old Dutch Cleanser to burnish the surface.

The most popular finish for baby shoes is dark bronze, and this is obtained by briefly immersing the shoe in a solution made of 3 ounces "Liver of Sulfur" dissolved in 1 gallon of water, used at room temperature. Keep the shoe in the solution until it turns a uniform dark brown color and then rinse in running water. Next, the shoe is highlighted by rubbing the naturally worn parts with the steel wool and cleanser. Generally it is finished by applying a coat of clear lacquer.

Silver or gold finishes are obtained by plating in those solutions over the copper instead of treating with liver of sulfur. For an "oxidized" silver finish, the shoe is plated with silver, and then treated with the liver of sulfur solution used hot, and highlighted as with the dark bronze finish.

Copper sulfate crystals may form on the anodes in time, and this is a sign that water has been lost. Restore the solution to its original volume occasionally by adding distilled water. For each baby shoe you plate, add a medicine dropper of sulfuric acid.

General Instructions

Stripping

This procedure is the reverse of plating; that is, the article to be stripped is the anode, and a piece of brass is used as the cathode, in the Electro Stripping Solution.

Stripping is used to remove old plating, and to brighten up oxidized surfaces and clean inaccessible places. The surface being treated may turn dark, due to the electrolytic action, and it may be necessary alternately to treat the article with the scratch brush and to return it to the stripping tank until the desired brightness is obtained.

Polishing Wheels and Compounds

Plating is generally only skin deep. It covers the work, colors it, protects it from corrosion, tarnish, and abrasion. But it does not fill in surface defects, such as pits and scratches, nor does it *polish* the work. The type of finish depends almost entirely on the preparation *before* plating. To brighten up new objects, generally a little buffing with rouge is all that is needed. For worn objects with surface corrosion or light scratches, a little cutting with tripoli is required. If the article is rough, or deeply scratched or gouged, it will probably have to be ground with emery. A scratch brush is also essential for cleaning the work, for producing mat surfaces, and for burnishing each layer when repeated deposits are desired.

The Nature of Plating Solutions

The kind of metal to be deposited is always contained in the plating solution. Direct current passing through the solution will cause the metal to be deposited on the cathode, or negative electrode.

In order to control the deposit so as to obtain the desired qualities of adherence, density, throwing power, luster, and color, a vast amount of electrochemical research has been required.

Fortunately this work has reached a high degree of success in solutions. They have been balanced chemically to give the desired results when used as directed.

Wearing Qualities

Up to now, we have discussed only flash plating which is extremely thin, but is thick enough to color and brighten jewelry. Since the metals deposited are soft (except rhodium) they may not be expected to stand much wear. But where the surface to be plated has a somewhat similar color, the color of the plating will persist for an unexpected duration. You can plate a 10-karat ring to a 14-karat color, and this color will persist for many months. Likewise, a gold filled watch case worn down to the brass base in spots can be gold plated, and a long time will elapse before the case will take on a brassy look. Even though the gold is extremely thin, it will blend in and give the surface uniform color.

Rubbing with the fingers has a polishing effect on such objects.

Articles that are not frequently handled should be protected with a coat of clear lacquer. Such articles include costume jewelry, compacts, and the like.

There is no limit to the thickness of metal that can be deposited. However, after the article has been in the plating solution for a prolonged period of time, let us say 5 or 10 minutes, the surface will become frosty and dull because of the formation of tiny nodules. The article should then be brought out and scratch brushed to burnish down the surface. It is again treated with the electrocleaner, rinsed, and returned to the plating bath; this cycle may be repeated as many times as desired.

Of course, it must be polished to the desired luster before the final plating.

The Life of Plating Solutions

Since metal is deposited out of the solution, this loss must be made up if the solution is to retain its original concentration or normal working strength. Such replacement may be effected by dissolving metal from a soluble anode in the plating operation itself; but when an insoluble anode is used (as in rhodium or palladium plating), the addition must be made in the form of a new solution.

The primary function of the anode, or positive electrode, is to introduce electric current into the bath. This causes the metal particles in the bath to be deposited on the negative electrode, or cathode, which is the article to be plated. Whenever possible, a soluble anode is used and it has been shown that the same amount of metal deposited at the cathode can be dissolved from the anode. Theoretically, a plating solution could be kept in balance this way so far as the metal concentration is concerned. In actual practice, this theory works out very well, and the use of the correct soluble anode will greatly prolong the life of the solution.

However, it must be taken into account that the chemicals will eventually be carried out by the articles being plated and that some deterioration will be caused by dust, so that eventually a solution will become unfit for use.

Although research has been exhaustive, no solutions have yet been formulated for plating rhodium or palladium with a soluble anode. Therefore, the strength of these baths must be maintained by the addition of fresh solution.

Care of Solutions

Plating solutions should be kept covered when not in use. Clock glasses are suitable for the 800 cc beakers. When not in daily use it is better to pour the solution back into the bottle or jug. In this way, it is easy to note the amount of water lost by evaporation, and this can be restored by filling the bottle with distilled water. Use only the anodes recommended, as the use of substitute anodes such as scrap gold will introduce impurities into the solution and render it unfit for use. Solutions should be filtered when the presence of dust or dirt is apparent. This is to prevent floating particles from settling on the work and causing spots.

Temperature

Although not always a highly critical factor, best results will be obtained by adhering to the recommended temperatures. An immersion thermometer, obtained from a photographic supply store is suitable for this purpose.

Care of the Plater

If your plater fails to operate, examine the fuse, using a screwdriver if necessary to unscrew the fuse holder. If burned out, it should be replaced with a 5 amp auto or radio fuse. Crossing the wires or allowing the anode to touch the cathode or overloading the plater will most certainly blow out the fuse, and you should have some extra ones on hand. Turn the switch off when the plater is not in use, particularly overnight.

The plater should last forever, so long as no moisture gets between the rectifier plates. This will never happen if the plater is used as often as once a month. Never store it away in a damp place, and if it is not in normal use turn the switch on for an hour or two once a month.

Metal Surfaces Requiring Special Treatment

Soft solder, lead, iron, and white metal do not readily lend themselves to plating with most metals. However, they can be successfully plated with copper. Therefore, plate first with copper, and then proceed as with any other job.

Chromium Plated Work

The best way to handle this is to remove the chromium by treating the article in a warm (110° F) solution of hydrochloric (also called "muriatic") acid, diluted 3 parts acid to 1 part water, until the chromium is all dissolved. In some cases the last vestiges of the chromium may not appear to be dissolved, but can readily be removed with the scratch brush. The underlying metal can then be plated in the usual way. Zinc-base die castings are rapidly attacked by hydrochloric acid, and such jobs are to be avoided. Hydrochloric acid will also attack iron and steel, but less rapidly, and articles containing steel parts should not be treated longer than absolutely necessary.

Stainless Steel

This must first be plated for 6 minutes in a stainless steel conditioner which is used at room temperature at 6 volts, with a pure nickel anode. The article is then plated with nickel and following this treatment, may be plated with gold or other metals.

Aluminum

Methods have been developed for plating on aluminum but we do not recommend the practice for about the same reasons we do not recommend chromium plating—except in the hands of an experienced, full-time plater.

Materials Harmed by Plating Solutions

Pearls—genuine, cultured, or imitation—shell cameos, mirror-back or foil-back stones, celluloid, imitation stones made of plastic or other plastic articles, turquoise, opals, and similar soft or nonheat-resistant materials may be attacked by plating solutions. Where they are present, do not attempt to plate the article unless you are willing to remove and replace them. Some articles, generally costume jewelry, are "set" with stones glued in with lacquer or cement. Plating might result is the stones' falling out.

"Soft enamel," which is really only paint, will soften and dissolve, and must be replaced after plating.

This does not mean that materials such as celluloid and plastics cannot be plated, but the surface must be properly treated, as described in the following directions for plating non-metallic objects, and unheated solutions must be used.

Plating Non-metallic Objects

There are two primary requirements. First, the object must be impervious to plating solutions. Second, it must be able to carry electric current.

Absorbent materials like wood, leather, etc. may be coated with shellac to make them impervious to those solutions which may be used at room temperature, such as copper or silver.

A conductive surface may be applied by coating the object with copper powder mixed with lacquer.

How To Do Larger Work

Two or more platers may be connected in parallel and the surface area which can be treated may be multiplied by the number of platers used.

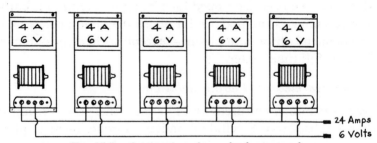

FIG. 15.5.   Connecting platers for larger work.

Fig. 15.5 shows how 6 platers connected in parallel will yield 24 amps at 6 volts. Similarly, 6 platers connected in series will yield 4 amps at 26 volts.

Plating Solutions

USE OF PLATING SOLUTIONS

Solution	Dilution Parts Solution	Parts Water	Temp.	Voltage	Maximum Area* Sq. Ins.
Copper	1	3	100° F	6	39
Electro cleaner	1	3	180° F	6	40
Electro stripping	1	3	180° F	6	40
Gold, any color	1	0	180° F	6	80
Nickel	1	0	70° F	2	48
Rhodium	1	0	110° F	6	39
Silver	1	3	70° F	2	238
Stainless steel conditioner	1	0	70° F	6	34
Chromium**			110° F	6	4
Copper (acid sulfate)**			70° F	6	240

* Number of square inches that can be processed with one Hoover Electro Plater operating at full nominal capacity of 4 amps, where the effective area of the anode equals the effective area of the cathode and the distance between anodes and cathodes is 2 inches.

** Solution not supplied by Hoover & Strong.

A list of necessary equipment and supplies as well as plating solutions available may be obtained by application to Hoover & Strong, Inc., Buffalo 1, New York.

Warnings

Solutions containing sodium cyanide or sodium hydroxide should be clearly labeled at all times. The label should be marked **DANGER** and **POISON** in a most conspicuous place. Keep both out of the reach of children.

Sodium Cyanide

Sodium cyanide may be fatal if swallowed. Contact with acid liberates poisonous gas. Avoid contact with skin and wash hands thoroughly after using. If ingested, call a physician immediately and start first aid treatment:

1. Remove victim to fresh air.

2. Break amyl nitrite pearl in a cloth and hold lightly under the patient's nose for 15 seconds.

3. If patient is conscious, induce vomiting by giving him a tablespoon of salt in a glass of warm water to drink.

4. Repeat inhalation of amyl nitrite at 5-minute intervals 5 times.

Sodium Hydroxide

Avoid contact with the skin, eyes, mucous membranes, and clothing, as sodium hydroxide causes severe burns.

For external contact, flush area with water for 15 minutes and then wash with vinegar.

If swallowed, have patient drink large quantities of milk or water followed by citrus juice or diluted vinegar. Call physician at once.

If a solution containing sodium hydroxide gets in someone's eyes, wash with water for 15 minutes and then get medical attention without delay.

Chapter 16

Solutions and Formulae

Antioxidizing solution
Pickle solution
Cleaning solutions
Tarnish remover
Removing mercury
Removing soft solder
Soft-soldering flux
Hard-solder flux
Testing silver
Testing gold
Determining the karat value of gold
Oxidizing solutions
Gilding
Working with acids
Satin finish
Lacquering
Pearl cement
Removing cement
Tinting and finishing solutions

IN SETTING UP a jewelry repair shop, all solutions, harmless or dangerous, should be clearly labeled, not only for reasons of safety, but also to obtain maximum efficiency in the department. Much time can be lost in searching for the right solution and valuable merchandise can be spoiled by using the wrong solution.

235

It is considered good practice to have all dangerous ingredients well out of reach of children or of employees who might not be aware of the potency of the contents of the many jars in the jewelry repair shop.

Another important factor to consider is adequate ventilation. Acid fumes from a faulty bottle or heavy ammonia fumes are hardly a contributing factor to an efficient day's work. Fumes such as these are damaging to health, especially if breathed daily, and *cyanide fumes can be deadly*. A jewelry repairman can grow so accustomed to breathing a polluted atmosphere that he is unaware of the true condition of the air in his shop.

Antioxidizing Solution

To 1 pint of denatured alcohol add as much boric acid as will dissolve. Before soldering, articles are dipped in the solution and ignited. The alcohol in the solution will burn out, leaving a protective coating or film that reduces discoloration during the soldering operation.

Pickle Solution

For a heated solution, mix 9 parts water with 1 part sulfuric acid. For a cold solution use 8 parts water with 2 parts sulfuric acid. The acid is always poured into the water to avoid a reaction.

After hard-soldering an article, place it in the pickle solution, using brass tweezers (steel tweezers will spoil the solution, causing it to plate). Allow the article to remain in the cold pickle solution for several minutes. Remove and wash off pickle solution under running water. A warm or hot solution will act much faster, and the article can be removed in a much shorter time. For removing pickle solution from large articles, place them in a warm solution of washing soda and water.

Cleaning Solutions

There are two stock solutions for general use.

STOCK SOLUTION #1

1 gallon water
2 ounces lump borax
1 ounce washing soda
15 pennyweight castile soap
5 fluid ounces aqua-ammonia (27-28%)

A small amount of this solution can be poured into a metal pan and placed over a burner. Articles to be cleaned may be boiled for a short time and scrubbed with a bristle brush if necessary, although any stone that may be damaged by heat should be scrubbed only, using the warm solution and a bristle brush. This type of article may be allowed to soak in a warm solution before brushing.

STOCK SOLUTION #2

1 ounce acetone
1 ounce oleic acid
14 ounces aqua-ammonia (27-28%)
<u>16 ounces water</u>
32 ounces or 1 quart

To make 1 gallon of Stock Solution #2, quadruple the quantities given for all the ingredients.

Obviously, this solution is reserved for the severely contaminated articles. Best results are obtained when the articles are allowed to soak for several minutes or longer.

Warning

This solution can remove the skin from the hands. Therefore, articles cleaned should be handled with tweezers and/or rubber gloves, and the fingers should never touch the solution. Some people are allergic to oleic acid or acetone. For those with an established allergy, this solution should be avoided unconditionally, as it may cause serious skin irritation.

Tarnish Remover

Allow one sodium cyanide egg to dissolve in one quart of water. Keep in a glass container with a glass lid. Mark the container **DEADLY POISON, CYANIDE** and keep it out of reach until ready to use. Dip the article for 15 to 20 seconds, using copper or brass wire to suspend it. Remove; rinse in running water, then alcohol.

Cyanide is also available in granular form. The proportion is 1 ounce to one pint of water.

Removing Mercury

Mercury may be removed on gold and silver jewelry by using nitric acid or by using heat. The nitric acid is applied by using the long glass stopper of the acid bottle, then rinsed off after a few seconds on the article. Sometimes the mercury may be removed by heating the article and polishing away the residue.

Removing Soft Solder

For silver and gold, immerse the article in muriatic acid. For other metals, the soft solder must be scraped off. For plated work, use Rex Soft Solder Remover, and boil in a copper pan.

Soft-soldering Flux

This can be made by dissolving a small amount of zinc chloride in alcohol. It can also be made by dissolving particles of zinc in muriatic acid until bubbling ceases, and then adding a small amount of sal ammoniac. Satisfactory fluxes may be obtained from material houses.

Hard-solder Flux

Stick borax rubbed on a borax slate, with a little water added to get a pastelike consistency, will provide such a flux. (See Solders and Fluxes in Chapter 3.)

Testing Silver

Place a drop of chromic acid on the article and place it under running water. If a red spot remains, the article is silver. If no color is seen, the article is not silver. If the silver content is lower than in coin silver, the color will be chocolate. If the article is sterling, the color will be a decided red. Silver may also be tested with nitric acid. File a notch deep enough to penetrate any plating and apply the acid with a small glass rod. The following reactions will be observed: If the article is of sterling silver, a cloudy cream color will show. If coin silver, a blackish foam will show. If plated silver, a greenish foam will show. Silver of grade 750 or lower will show different shades of green, darkening as the silver content is lowered.

Testing Gold

With a small file, make a nick on the article deep enough to penetrate plating, and apply nitric acid. The following reactions will be observed: if the article is of gold plate over base metal, a bright green reaction will result. If gold plated over silver, a pinkish cream color will show. Ten-karat gold will show a slight reaction; over 10-karat gold shows little or no reaction.

Determining the Karat Value of Gold

First rub the article on the testing stone. Rub two or three needles of the estimated karat near the mark made by the article. The acid will cause a reaction on all marks. The correct karat is determined when like reactions are found between the needle mark and the article mark. The reaction will be simultaneous.

Use nitric acid for 10-karat gold or less, and aqua regia for anything above 10-karat gold.

Oxidizing Solutions

For oxidizing silver, use a solution of Liver of Sulfur (potassium sulfide) and water, and apply it to the article with a camel's-hair brush and heat until the surface turns black. Then brush off with a stiff brush and rub off high parts with pumice stone.

For oxidizing copper use liver of sulfur (potassium sulfide). The solution should be: 1 ounce liver of sulfur to 1 quart hot water. Add less than half an ounce of ammonia. Apply as explained above for oxidizing silver.

To oxidize brass apply butter of antimony (antimony chloride solution) to the article and allow to dry.

To oxidize gold, first heat the article. With a camel's-hair brush, apply a warm ammonium sulfide solution, rinse the article, and polish. To make ammonium sulfide solution, add ammonium sulfide to water until the solution turns pale yellow in color. Always warm solution before using.

Gilding

There are on the market today many satisfactory plating outfits that are comparatively inexpensive. Results are satisfactory, quick, and generally superior to other methods. However, gilding can be done by making up your own solution.

Add 1 pint chloride of gold to 2 pints distilled water. Add 16 ounces potassium bicarbonate. Heat the mixture for an hour, never allowing it to boil. Immerse the thoroughly clean article in the warm solution until the desired color is seen.

Chloride of gold is made by dissolving 6 pennyweight of gold in 1 pint of acid mixture. This acid mixture contains equal parts of muriatic acid and nitric acid.

It is well to gild many repair jobs at the completion of the washing and drying operation. This will give the work a lustrous appearance which is very pleasing to the owner, although its durability is not permanent.

Working with Acids

Great caution should be exercised in working with acids. Acid containers may be of glass or crockery, but must be coated with black asphaltum varnish. (This can be bought at all paint stores.) It is safer to use rubber gloves around acids. Should any acid come in contact with the skin, an instant neutralizer is soda or ammonia, which is generally on hand in any jewelry workshop. While working around acids, be sure that there is good ventilation. Also have jars or containers well labeled as a warning to anyone unfamiliar with jewelry-shop methods.

Satin Finish

Dip the article into a solution containing 1 part hydrofluoric acid and 3 parts water.

Lacquering

To lacquer small articles, use a soft camel's-hair brush. Secure a good grade of clear lacquer and thin it in a separate jar, using lacquer thinner. The proper amount of thinner depends on the consistency of the lacquer. Generally a half-and-half mixture is satisfactory. It should be applied by brushing on quickly with a single stroke. Do not be tempted to brush over certain areas to smooth out ripples. If properly thinned and applied, the lacquer will smooth itself without continued brushing. If the job is unsatisfactory, remove immediately with lacquer thinner, clean and dry the article; lacquer again. The article must always be clean and dry; lacquer and thinner solution must be free of any foreign matter; and the brush must be clean and soft. Do not lacquer where dust is apt to settle on the work.

Lacquering prevents tarnish and preserves finish. It is used to better advantage on articles that receive very little handling. It is useless to lacquer any piece of jewelry that receives constant wear, for the lacquer will wear off in spots, exposing the metal.

Pearl Cement

Gum mastic, which hardens very quickly, is very satisfactory for cementing pearls on pegs, etc.

Removing Cement

To remove cement from articles, either wood or grain alcohol may be used. Simply immerse the article in the alcohol and allow the cement to dissolve.

Tinting and Finishing Solutions

To bronze-finish copper, make a solution of 1 ounce potassium sulfocyanide and 3 ounces iron nitrate dissolved in 2 quarts water. Apply with cotton or submerge the article in the solution. Remove, dry, and lacquer.

To give copper a gray color, make a solution of 2 ounces arsenic chloride in 1 quart water. Submerge the article in the hot solution, dry, and lacquer.

To brown-finish copper, dissolve 1 pint of white vinegar, $\frac{2}{3}$ ounce potassium oxalate, and 2 ounces sal ammoniac. Apply with cotton or submerge the article in the solution, dry, and lacquer.

To bronze-tint brass, make a solution of $\frac{3}{4}$ pound potassium nitrate and 1 pint sulfuric acid. Add to this $\frac{1}{2}$ gill nitric acid and $\frac{1}{2}$ gill hydrochloric acid. Submerge, dry, and lacquer.

To green-tint brass, make a solution using $\frac{1}{4}$ pound sal ammoniac and $\frac{1}{4}$ pound copper sulfate to 1 quart boiling water. Apply with a stiff brush and allow to dry.

To gray-tint brass, make a solution of 1 ounce arsenic chloride in 1 pint water. Submerge the article, dry, and lacquer.

Chapter 17

Buying Supplies and Findings

RATHER THAN try to present an exhaustive list of all supplies and findings, our discussion here will endeavor to point out the most important factors in purchasing difficult or perplexing items.

For example, a simple wire ring guard (Fig. 17.1) is an item that has been used for years in all jewelry stores. The question still remains concerning the quality to use—gold or gold filled or both. It is normally assumed that a 14-karat diamond ring should have a solid gold ring guard at a retail cost of approximately $2.00-$3.50. In many stores a plated ring guard would not be considered for the job. Yet, in another store, the maximum price the customer will pay may be only $.75 to $1.50. The answer, of course, is the gold-filled ring guard. There are stores that do not carry ring guards at all, but will size the ring for the customer instead, believing this to be the only satisfactory way to handle the situation.

Of course, there are customers who will insist they do not want the ring cut and apparently a ring guard sale is lost in this store. One thing to consider, and this is not to reflect in any way on the quality of gold-filled ring guards, the gold will eventually wear through to the base metal at which time discoloration may be apparent. This can be viewed either as an opportunity to sell another ring guard or as a possible dissatisfied customer who will register a complaint.

Wire ring guards are usually bought on cards of one dozen assorted sizes. There are usually six different sizes. If the smallest sizes move faster than the largest ones, then cards may be purchased containing sizes 1 to 3 only.

243

There are a number of designs in ring guards, and it is not our intention to favor any particular one over the other. Rather, our purpose here is to discuss impartially what appears to be most in demand.

There has been a growing demand for a ring guard of a heavier design than the common wire type, one that covers a range considerably wider. See Fig. 17.2 for a general idea of the design. This

FIG. 17.1.   A wire ring guard.

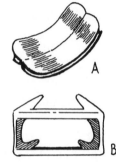

A

B

FIG. 17.3.   Ring locks or clasps.

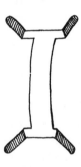

FIG. 17.2.   Heavier ring guard.

style may be bought to fit the largest man's ring as well as a narrow lady's ring.

Also in popular demand are the ring locks, devices for holding wedding band and engagement ring together. (See Fig. 17.3.) There are several designs offered, and this item should be included in the stock of a beginning jeweler—not necessarily in large quantity but in a range of sizes in both white and yellow.

The purchase of gold sizing stock deserves considerable thought and planned buying. For large manufacturing houses, trade repair-men, and stores with adequate jewelry repair volume, many sizes, shapes, and karats are necessary, involving quite an investment in gold. (See Fig. 17.4A, B, C.) While having such a supply and range to choose from would be helpful to the small jeweler, the invest-ment is usually prohibitive, and the full range is not absolutely necessary. If one had a size of gold stock in a dimension large enough to accommodate all widths, thicknesses, and shapes, the investment in gold stock would be out of proportion to the volume

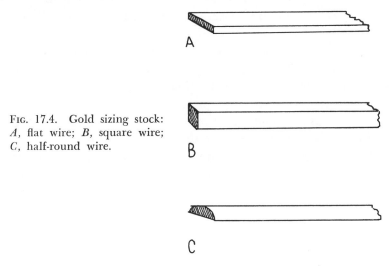

FIG. 17.4. Gold sizing stock: *A*, flat wire; *B*, square wire; *C*, half-round wire.

of work being done. With a flat piece of stock 6 × 2 mm, the ma-jority of ring sizing assignments (men's rings and ladies') can be accomplished with little waste. It is, however, advisable to have two different stock sizes: 2 × 1½ mm for ladies' rings and 6 × 2 mm for men's. This will save time in sizing ladies' rings, for on shank jobs, particularly, the task of sawing the length out of the 6 × 2 mm is too time-consuming.

The 2 × 1½ mm width is used more than the 6 × 2 mm width. Hence, if one has exhausted the supply of the smaller stock tem-porarily, one can still complete a sizing job with the 6 × 2 mm piece, which provides the required thickness, without delay.

The following coverage is usually adequate for the average jewelry store: 6 × 2 mm 10-karat yellow stock, 6 × 2 mm 14-karat yellow stock, 2 × 1½ mm 10-karat yellow stock, 2 × 1½ mm 14-karat yellow stock, 6 × 2 mm 14-karat white gold stock, and 2 × 1½ mm 14-karat white gold stock—all sizes in a flat shape. One can see how large one's investment would be if one were to stock all sizes and shapes in 10-karat, 14-karat, and 18-karat stock.

Of course, the flat shape suggested here means some extra filing work, but no real loss of gold, since filings are caught in the lap drawer and salvaged. As the old master jewelers used to say, "You can always file *away* excess metal, but it's awfully hard to file it *on*."

Many beginners feel that the half-round stock is obviously the sensible and time-saving way to buy gold stock—that is, until they are presented with a ring sizing job in which the curvature of the shank does not conform to the curvature of the sizing stock. (See Fig. 17.4C.) The error is obvious immediately, and stock of a larger or fuller shape is then obtained. In purchasing solders, the range should at least be equivalent to the stock (gold) on hand—10-karat, 14-karat, in yellow and 14-karat in white. Even though no sizing stock is carried in 18-karat yellow or 10-karat and 18-karat white, it is well to have the solders on hand. Frequently jobs will come up where it is advisable to match the solder exactly with the quality of gold. Mismatching of the karat of solder to the karat of gold may not be too noticeable as soon as the job is completed, but characteristically it shows up later and very obviously.

One solder frequently overlooked is the low-karat gold solder which may be used to good advantage where a low heat is desired. Repair jobs often turn up where it is necessary to solder very close to a previous joint. By using a low-karat solder the job may be completed without disturbing the other joint.

Silver solder should always be on hand, being useful for a number of miscellaneous hard-soldering operations.

The soft solders, lead or bismuth, are a very necessary item being useful in repairing metals that will not withstand the intense heat of hard soldering.

Different fluxes are required for hard solders and soft solders, a fact which seems scarcely worth mentioning—or at least fairly obvious. However, beginning repairmen have attempted to hard solder with soft-solder flux and vice versa.

Swivels are a fairly easy item to purchase, the usual quality being a good grade of gold filled. They are generally available in about four sizes suitable for 18S, 16S and 12S watches. The fourth smaller size may be used for any odd size movement smaller than 12S. It is advisable to carry all sizes in stock with the emphasis on the yellow swivels.

There are other designs in higher-grade swivels, one of the most popular being used on railroad type watches. This design has a screw top that locks the spring-loop section. This style can be added to regular stock if a demand for it exists.

There are cheaper grades of swivels available and there is a demand for them in some sections. Due to customer resistance to the price of gold-filled swivels, some jewelers feel forced to carry the cheaper grade in addition to the gold-filled quality. One word of caution—it is not good policy to use cheap findings, for the few pennies saved will not compensate for the customer good will that can so easily be lost. Cheap findings may look as good as quality gold-filled findings when delivered to the customer. The durability of the finish is surprisingly short by comparison, however. The customers may never come back to complain—they may never come back at all, but may instead go to another store and insist on a quality product. The overall risk of using poor quality findings is too great.

Spring rings are one of the most frequently replaced findings. The range of sizes is very wide and since they must be carried in both white and yellow, the investment in spring rings can be comparatively heavy. However, this item may be considered almost in the same category as regular merchandise, for the profit in selling a spring ring is certainly good, and the time involved in installing it is usually negligible. Therefore, it would seem wise to have an adequate stock on hand at all times and to reorder immediately when stock runs low. To simplify stock control, many supply houses offer little systems or cabinets arranged from small to large, with stock numbers on individual containers. To start with such a cabinet would save a lot of time and would certainly forestall a "where-did-I-put-those-large-spring-rings" crisis.

There are generally two designs of spring rings to be considered. See Fig. 17.5. Even though the quality of the two may be the same,

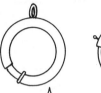

FIG. 17.5. Spring rings: *A*, lip type; *B*, pin type.

the pin type is frequently the more expensive, due to the design. The lip type is very simple to operate, but sometimes has the disadvantage of being too bulky to engage itself properly in the jump ring. To overcome this, the pin type spring ring serves well. The lip is eliminated and the spring section is operated by using a pin that slides back and forth in a race. In addition to these extra features, the pin is threaded and screws into position.

Of course, the pin type is not essential on all jobs and, if one is to decide between the two styles, let us say that the smallest sizes usually cause the trouble with the lip type. The pin type has no substitute in the small range, unless, of course, it is possible to use a larger jump ring to accommodate the lip style. Often, a chain is too small to use a larger jump ring, and enough time may be saved by using the pin type to more than make up the difference in price.

Spring rings can also be bought in less expensive qualities, but the advisability of using them is even more questionable than using a cheap grade of swivel. Spring rings are usually worn where they are seen and a darkened spring ring is too obvious. Quality gold-filled is safest.

There are frequent requests for solid gold spring rings in the smaller sizes. Many neck chains are of solid gold and the customer may insist on having a solid gold spring ring. If the demand is low the jeweler may not wish to stock these but can easily obtain them as needed from his supplier.

Sterling spring rings are also available and may be stocked. However, the emphasis should be on the white and yellow gold filled. If out of sterling, it is far better to use a white-gold-filled spring ring on a sterling chain than to use a sterling spring ring on a white gold-filled chain. This may be splitting hairs somewhat, but a difference of color can easily show up on the sterling spring ring after it is worn.

Jump rings are a very necessary item, one that should always be in stock in every imaginable size. These may be had in all qualities, and much care should be used in selecting the right quality. They are available in small assortments, making reordering simple by using stock numbers for each size. Hence, when low on one size, it is not necessary to reorder another complete assortment.

Necklace clasps for 1-strand, 2-strand, and 3-strand beads may be stocked in minimum quantity with emphasis on the 1-strand. These are generally stocked in sterling but are also available in solid gold. Even if bead stringing is not to be done on the premises, the replacement of a clasp is an easy task and a frequent one.

There are a variety of styles of bead clasps especially in the rhinestone category. Unless the demand is especially great for this type it is better to order these as needed. For any rare type of clasp it is best to send the sample to the supplier for matching.

If bead stringing is to be done on the premises, the best way to begin is by purchasing an assortment of bead cord (with needles attached). The assortment will contain more of the most-used sizes and coverage on the least-used sizes. From this the sizes may be reordered on an individual basis. The cord and the needle may be ordered separately, but the most popular way is to order the bead cord with needle attached. Nylon has increased in popularity, whereas the silk quality has diminished.

Bead tips are a very necessary part of bead stringing, and an adequate supply should always be on hand. This is a frequently overlooked item.

Index